Avoiding #FAIL

Mitigating Risk, Managing Threats and Protecting The Corporation in the Age of Social Media

Stephen J. Andriole
Vincent J. Schiavone
Erika von Hoyer
Mark D. Langsfeld
Mark R. Harrington

© 2013 Ascendigm Press

Avoiding #FAIL
Mitigating Risk, Managing Threats and Protecting The
Corporation in the Age of Social Media
First Edition, hardcover – published 2013
Ascendigm Press
ISBN: 978-0-9887311-3-4

10 9 8 7 6 5 4 3 2 1

Avoiding #FAIL

Mitigating Risk, Managing Threats and
Protecting the Corporation
in the Age of Social Media

Contents

Avoiding #FAIL

Mitigating Risk, Managing Threats and Protecting the Corporation in the Age of Social Media

Acknowledgements

All books are team efforts. This one is no exception. First, there are analysts that look, listen and infer – day in and day out. They are a hearty bunch that seldom buckle under the social spigot that's on all the time. The ListenLogic analysts worked tirelessly to generate the cases presented in the book. Thank you for excellent work.

Without technology, there's no social business intelligence. The Akuda Labs and ListenLogic technology teams that make collection, classification, analysis and reporting possible are – like the analysts who use their technology – the other half of the delivery team that enable social business and social risk intelligence. Our technologists have invented whole new ways to cost-effectively collect, classify and analyze big social data. We thank them for their creative work.

Stephen J. Andriole
Vincent J. Schiavone
Erika von Hoyer
Mark D. Langsfeld
Mark R. Harrington

Preface

As the requirement to "go social" increases, the risks of going social *badly* also rise.

Less than 2% of *Fortune* 500 CEOs are actively engaged on Twitter today – and likely for good reason. Although it's tempting for chief executives to jump on to the social bandwagon to help personify their company, increase perceived consumer accessibility or simply appearing like an industry pioneer, doing so without understanding the dangers of the social megaphone is extremely dangerous to the personal reputations of the executives, company brands and even revenue.

A case-in-point is Mark Bertolini, Aetna's Chief Executive Officer. Bertolini jumped onto the social bandwagon in September 2009, veiling his identity and only posting personal musings to family and friends, initially anonymous to the general public. After his appointment as CEO in November 2011, the company encouraged him to unveil his identity on Twitter to provide "a face" to the Aetna organization. Bertolini agreed and subsequently posted a blend of personal and professional tweets. However, what initially appeared to be a harmless endeavor to put "a face" on the Aetna brand, quickly exploded into an embarrassing public battle with a policy-holding cancer patient, resulting in an inadvertently changed corporate policy and ultimately an impact to shareholder value – *all from a handful of tweets*.

The blessing and curse for Bertolini and other high-profile executives is that social media serves as a direct channel with anyone at anytime, providing engagement *and exposure*. While this can certainly provide value to corporations if properly controlled, it also introduces tremendous risk to their operations as Bertolini and Aetna learned all too well.

As social media becomes a mainstay tool for businesses, many organizations are attracted by the potential to broadcast to wide audiences. However, the challenge for these companies is to maintain message control and define policies that address threats and mitigate risks. It's an even larger challenge to have their executives understand and consistently adhere to these rules.

The need for control is not unlike the approach corporations have with press conferences where they manage the forum and the message. Increasingly, executives become complacent in their social media interactions due to the informal, the easy nature of the "channels," lowering their guard and seemingly forgetting that their accounts are essentially broadcasting media.

Companies need a deep understanding and appreciation of the social media channels they're engaging and a strong discipline to maintain control of their comments in order to protect and advance their corporate brands and avoid embarrassing situations while adhering to corporate policy designed to avoid damaging their corporate brands or – worse – reducing shareholder value. Although it's well known that many social users will attempt to attack, bait or embarrass well-known personas, self-inflicted damage also occurs when self-discipline recedes and emotion rules.

Executives that fail to understand and appreciate the growing threats of the online social world, greatly increase the potential of reputational and financial risk to their companies and ultimately their shareholders.

Simply put, social media is media. Media rules fully apply and companies must equate social media broadcasting to an open mic at a press conference (or political fund raiser).

The baiting approach and the resulting natural 'twitch' response is largely what sparked the very public Twitter battle between Mark Bertolini (@mtbert) and Arijit Guha (@Poop_Strong).

Guha, a 31 year-old Ph.D. student fighting stage IV colon cancer was also battling mounting medical bills that surpassed the $300,000 cap from his Aetna policy provided through the University of Arizona, leaving him with $118,000 in out-of-pocket expenses.

Fighting to avoid financial ruin, Guha kicked off PoopStrong.com, a campaign to raise funds and awareness for his plight and to also advocate for healthcare insurance reform.

Through a small core of well-connected supporters, Guha quickly surpassed his fundraising goal. Despite this success, however, he remained deeply motivated to voice his discontent with the policies of the insurance industry generally and Aetna specifically. To do this, he aggressively engaged Bertolini with several direct, attacking tweets seemingly with the intent to bait him into an online fight, including:

> *"@mtbert Moreover, do you think it's morally justifiable to offer a flawed insurance product that doesn't cover catastrophes?"*

> *"@mtbert @AetnaHelp And you could do more to help if you were more interested in helping than profit-maximizing."*

> *"In 2011, @Aetna CEO @mtbert "earned" $10.6 million in total compensation. Or $80k more PER WEEK than the bills Aetna's left me to pay."*

It worked.

Bertolini quickly responded to Guha's initial attacks with a pointed, seemingly sarcastic response, tweeting:

> *"@Poop_Strong @aetnahelp False. Why do you think the premium was so low? Do u look at your policy limits when u buy other insurance (auto)?"*

This resulted in Guha and a variety of his supporters pouncing on Bertolini's response. To counter, Bertolini attempted to "educate" his online adversaries on how the industry works in terms of aspects like costs and premiums.

It didn't work.

Making matters worse, Bertolini displayed his lack of online savvy with the "f/u" reference, presumably meant to indicate "follow up" but one that certainly could have been taken another way, particularly in the midst of a heated exchange.

"We are working to come up with a solution. We will f/u w/@Poop_Strong. The system is broken. I'm trying to fix it."

Social media has changed the dynamic of "influencers." Individuals do not need fame, fortune or followers to become influential in the social media universe. Strategic inclusion of media handles in posts and the smart use of hashtags can quickly result in massive exposure.

In the same tweet Bertolini also admits that the entire insurance industry system is broken and repeatedly states that he is on a campaign to fix it. Noble to be sure, but probably not the ideal message delivery channel or timing with a message that potentially undermines the actions of various groups across his organization like Aetna Customer Service (@AetnaHelp) tasked with customer engagement and satisfaction.

Beyond this, Bertolini publicly declared full support of his comments by his Board of Directors:

"Gregg, my public comments are informed by our strategy to find a better way. Our strategy is wholly endorsed by our BOD."

His comments may well have been "wholly endorsed" by the Aetna Board of Directors (BOD), but this seems to raise significant questions regarding a blanket endorsement of his Twitter posts by the Aetna Board of Directors. This introduces unnecessary risk resulting from a single tweet.

Interactions of this severity should be taken offline. As tempting as it is to respond via social media as Bertolini did, it has to be understood that in that venue the entire public is watching. Taking it offline allows companies to address the individual's issues privately without taking an inadvertent misstep for millions to see.

Ultimately, after a drawn out fight, Bertolini openly agreed to have Aetna cover Guha's balance of outstanding medical bills of $118,000. As Guha (@Poop_Strong) tweeted regarding this victory:

"Congrats, Twitter hordes! @Aetna just agreed to cover the full extent of my bills. Every last penny. Thanks, @mtbert, for listening."

To which Bertolini responded:

"@Poop_Strong I am glad we connected today and got this issue solved. I appreciate the dialog no matter how pointed. I've got it and own it!"

However, despite the noble nature of the response, this public decision by Bertolini to pay Guha's medical bill balance set a precedent and essentially transformed Aetna policy indicating that the company would cover student, if not all policy holder, medical bill balances not covered by their Aetna insurance policy.

As a result, many other policy-holder inquiries asking for similar results got tweeted to Bertolini and Aetna, pointing to the results of the Guha decision, like:

"@mtbert @Poop_Strong well done, but now what happens to everyone else without Twitter whose insurance has capped them just the same?"

"@mtbert I hope you can look at doing the same for others. No one should go broke b/c they get sick."

"I'm happy @aetna & @mtbert agreed to help @poop_strong, but in my own experience they've wrongly denied 6 of my claims in less than 3 years ... "

This single public declaration set a precedent, at least in the eyes of those watching, like the financial press, lawyers and plaintiffs, that Aetna will now cover the extended costs of policy holders once their cap is hit. Many consumers are not likely to view this public declaration as a one-off case or even one limited to college students. The precedent set by Bertolini suggests that if you don't get what you want from Aetna, circle up your "Twitter horde" (as Guha put it) and attack the CEO until you get what Guha got.

While this may seem like a case of the big, hulking corporation versus the small, powerless customer, this was really a situation where Guha and his "horde" played Goliath given their online savvy and aggressive tactics. Bertolini was David given his novice understanding of social media and lack of online discipline.

Guha's ability to generate pressure on a *Fortune 100* CEO and Bertolini's lack of social savvy and discipline, resulted in Aetna paying Guha's outstanding bill, but also pushed Bertolini into a publicly embarrassing situation and one where he restated Aetna policy to the masses by setting a precedent with one policy holder.

Just look at the social map in Figure 1.

Millions upon millions of participants are engaged in this conversation. Companies must understand just how viral communications can be – and how quickly news and commentary travels. Once out, there's no controlling good *or* bad news. Bad, controversial or scary news travels faster than good news.

The number of groups, influencers and re-tweeters is staggering – especially when one considers how fast all this came together. The map in Figure 1 paints an influence and communications picture of the Aetna social media debacle. Note the participants: the press, the government, the healthcare industry, activists, advocates and even the entertainment industry. This discussion was pervasive and jumped across vertical industries and the fourth estate – and then back again.

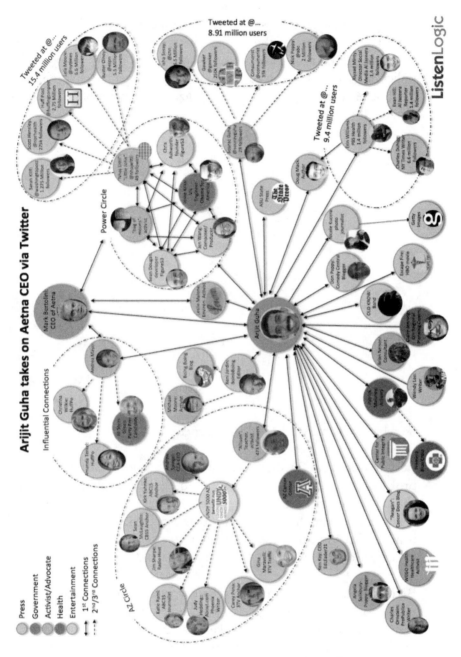

Figure 1: The Aetna/Guha Social Map

On top of it all, Aetna's stock saw a significant dip during the same period. The extent of the public Twitter war on this is debatable, but it's hard to argue that the social conversation with a disgruntled policy-holder that involved millions of participants and followers did not have an impact on the organization's shareholder value on potentially several levels.

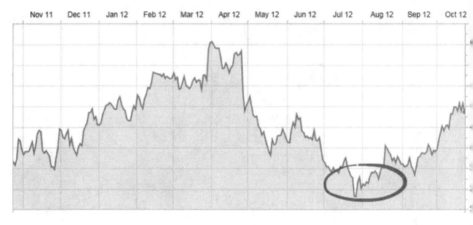

Nov 11   Dec 11   Jan 12   Feb 12   Mar 12   Apr 12   May 12   Jun 12   Jul 12   Aug 12   Sep 12   Oct 12

Poop Strong/Aetna
Twitter War

So what are some of the lessons learned?

Bertolini used his Twitter account to post a blend of personal and professional messages. Accounts used for professional messaging should be limited to the professional. Most followers of executives are interested in the CEO's company, not their favorite baseball team or fast food franchise. Mixing messages causes confusion and results in lowered guard by the executive.

Bertolini's major initial mistake was not addressing Guha's situation offline on a one-on-one basis. He had no way of winning in the court of public opinion, particularly when those in the court could publicly attack his every response. Bertolini also misunderstood and misinterpreted the public's general attitude toward healthcare costs and for-profit healthcare insurance companies: very few Americans believe that healthcare CEOs deserve $10,000,000 per year (or more) in total compensation when – pre "Obamacare" – 50,000,000 Americans live without healthcare.

Bertolini initially blasted back with a sarcastic, snarky question in response to Guha's aggressive attacks asking him if he actually "looked at his policy." This tweet set the stage for the extended battle, firing up Guha and his supporters even more.

Bertolini seemingly used the abbreviation "f/u" innocently meaning "follow up," but a lack of understanding of the common alternative meaning exacerbated the situation.

Perhaps it was the correct messaging for Bertolini to state that the "system is broken," but again the exchange was not the right approach for Bertolini to do so publicly.

Bertolini also claimed full support of the Aetna Board, which may be true but is risky and raises legal and liability questions given the volatile, unpredictable nature of Twitter and what can easily and mistakenly be said on the social channel.

With one single decision and subsequent tweet Bertolini transformed the perceived policy of Aetna potentially resulting in hundreds of millions of additional costs.

Executives have to appreciate the power of social media. They have to understand the impact that 140 characters can have on multi-billion dollar organizations. As tempting as it may be for executives to jump on to the social media bandwagon, they have to understand what the social channels represent – *a real-time global megaphone.*

Mark Bertolini made some missteps. The public spectacle resulted in restating Aetna's policy, resulting in massive additional costs for the company. The event also resulted in damaging Aetna's brand and reputation. In either case, regardless of Bertolini's intent and actions, shareholder value was at least temporarily damaged.

If only the Aetna case were an isolated event. Unfortunately, there are hundreds of these cases. We present 100 of them here. We also analyze them and suggest how to avoid bad social media, predict crises and how to reduce or eliminate social risks. Make no mistake, this is real business. The world's newest – *and by far largest* – communications channel is good, bad and – at times – very ugly. Companies must understand and manage this channel very, very carefully. *Avoiding #FAIL* will help you navigate the potentially very troubled waters of the social conversation.

In today's social age, #fail is the most dangerous hashtag to your business. An indication of deep contempt or displeasure with something, often a brand or business, #fail is used to broadcast corporate issues ranging from enterprise missteps, product liabilities, poor customer experiences or employee misconduct, among countless other situations. The #fail hashtag often helps these issues blossom into crises with immediate reach to millions of consumers and is consistently among the most used hashtags across the open social media universe and one that companies desperately try to avoid.

Stephen J. Andriole
Vincent J. Schiavone
Erika von Hoyer
Mark D. Langsfeld
Mark R. Harrington

Chapter 1 - Social Business Intelligence[1]

Wikipedia describes social media as:

"... media designed to be disseminated through social interaction, created using highly accessible and scalable publishing techniques. Social media uses Internet and web-based technologies to transform broadcast media monologues (one-to-many) into social media dialogues (many to many). It supports the democratization of knowledge and information, transforming people from content consumers into content producers. Businesses refer to social media as user-generated content (UGC) or consumer-generated media (CGM).

"Social media can take many different forms, including Internet forums, weblogs, social blogs, wikis, podcasts, pictures, video, rating and bookmarking. Technologies include: blogs, picture-sharing, vlogs, wall-postings, email, instant messaging, music-sharing, crowdsourcing, and voice over IP, to name a few.

"Social media have been modernized to reach consumers through the Internet. Social media have become appealing to big and small businesses. Credible brands are utilizing social media to reach customers and to build or maintain reputation. As social media continue to grow, the ability to reach more consumers globally has also increased.

"Twitter, for example has expanded its global reach to Japan, Indonesia, and Mexico, among others. This means that brands are now able to advertise in multiple languages and therefore reach a broader range of consumers. Social media have become the new "tool" for effective business marketing and

---

[1]Portions of Chapter 1 are drawn from Stephen J. Andriole, Vincent J. Schiavone, Luis F. Stevens, Mark D. Langsfeld and Mark R. Harrington, *Social Business Intelligence: Reducing Risk, Building Brands, Driving Growth with Social Media,* Ascendigm Press, 2013.

[1]Portions of Chapter 1 are drawn from Stephen J. Andriole, Vincent J. Schiavone, Luis F. Stevens, Mark D. Langsfeld and Mark R. Harrington, *Social Business Intelligence: Reducing Risk, Building Brands, Driving Growth with Social Media,* Ascendigm Press, 2013.

sales. Popular networking sites including Myspace, Facebook and Twitter are most commonly used for socialization and connecting friends, relatives, and employees."

Social media is the natural extension of old communications artifacts like email, instant messaging, bulletin boards, chat and eRooms. It's also the end-result of pervasive computing, the "always on" phenomenon that became reality in the early 2000s.

Social media is about participation – by anyone. It reflects the democratization of computing, a movement that levels the computing and communications playing field. It's also fueled by "consumerization," where technology innovation and adoption is driven by requirements and preferences that originate with consumers (and consumer vendors) rather than cubicle-constrained professionals and their rigid corporate technology providers.

Social media is about generational differences. Gen X and Y ("Millennials") are comfortable with technology (Gen X) and even excited about it (Gen Y): Millennials are, in fact, immersed in technology and assume IT. Gen Z, or "Zippies," don't even see technology as separate or unique. Those born after 2000 will challenge all of our ideas about technology adoption and optimization. Or, put another way, there'll be no need to study how quickly Zippies adopt technology or how well they use IT (information technology). IT will simply just be there the same way that chairs and toasters are there. *(Note the "official" dates for each era are as follows: 2000/2001-Present = Generation Z; 1980-2000 = Millennials or Generation Y; 1965-1979 = Generation X; 1946-1964 = Baby Boomers; 1925-1945 = Silent Generation; and 1900-1924 = G.I. Generation.)*

The key differences among the generations are behavioral – not technological. Millennials and obviously Zippies think nothing of sharing all sorts of personal information with their peers and even others in their spheres of communication and collaboration. In fact, definitions of "sharing," "personal" and "privacy" have all but converged: the younger you are the less offended you are about the semi-nude digital pictures taken – and posted for all to see – on Spring break.

Technology has enabled all this but make no mistake: social media is as much about behavioral changes as it is about always-on pervasive computing. The perfect storm of consumerization, technology capabilities and generational behavioral trends has delivered social media. Companies now must determine what they should do with social media. They have no choice. It's the new channel of the early 21st century. Social media represents one of the most profound changes – and opportunities – that we've ever seen in the way business works.

The Range of Social Media

Wikipedia provides a list of social media applications (at this point in time). The number changes on an almost daily basis. The number of social media applications – and the creative use of user-created content – is changing as our understanding of social media evolves and as our creativity about social media applications grows.

Examples (from Wikipedia) of social media applications include:

Communication

- **Blogs:** *WordPress, Blogger, BlogHer, Drupal, ExpressionEngine, LiveJournal, Open Diary, TypePad, Vox, Xanga*

- **Microblogging:** *Dailybooth, FMyLife, Google Buzz, Identi.ca, Jaiku, Nasza-Klasa.pl, Plurk, Posterous, Qaiku, Tumblr*

- **Engagement Advertising & Monetization:** *SocialVibe*

- **Location-Based Social Networks:** *Facebook places, Foursquare, Geoloqi, Google Latitude, Gowalla, The Hotlist, Yelp, Inc.*

- **Events:** *Eventful, The Hotlist, Facebook, Upcoming, Yelp, Inc.*

3

- **Information Aggregators:** *Netvibes, Twine (website)*

- **Online Advocacy & Fundraising:** *Causes, Jumo, Kickstarter, IndieGoGo*

- **Social N**etworking: *Facebook, Twitter, Pinterest, Instagram, Bebo, Chatter, Cyworld, Diaspora, Google+, Hi5, Hyves, IRC, LinkedIn, Mixi, MySpace, Netlog, Ning, Orkut, Plaxo, Tagged, Tuenti, XING, Yammer*

Collaboration/Authority Building

- **Collaboration:** *Central Desktop*

- **Content Management Systems:** *WordPress, Blogspot, E107 (CMS), Drupal, Joomla, Plone*

- **Diagramming & Visual Collaboration:** *Creately*

- **Document Managing & Editing Tools:** *Docs.com, Dropbox.com, Google Docs, Syncplicity*

- **Social Bookmarking (or Social Tagging):** *CiteULike, Delicious, Diigo, Google Reader, StumbleUpon, folkd, Zotero*

- **Social Media Gaming:** *Zynga, Empire Avenue*

- **Social Navigation:** *Trapster, Waze*

- **Social News:** *Digg, Stumble Upon, Chime.In* (formerly *Mixx*), *Newsvine, NowPublic, Reddit*

- **Research/Academic Collaboration:** *Mendeley, Zotero*

- **Wikis:** *PBworks, Wetpaint, Wikia, Wikidot, Wikimedia, Wikispaces, Wikinews*

Entertainment

- **Game Sharing:** *Zynga. Armor Games, Kongregate, Miniclip, Newgrounds*

- **Media & Entertainment Platforms:** *YouTube, MySpace, Cisco Eos, mtv.com*

- **Virtual Worlds:** *Second Life, Active Worlds, Forterra Systems, The Sims Online, World of Warcraft, RuneScape*

Multimedia

- **Livecasting:** *YouTube, Skype, Ustream, blip.tv, Justin.tv, Livestream, oovoo, OpenCU, Stickam*

- **Music & Audio Sharing:** *Pandora Radio, GrooveShark, Spotify, Guvera, Bandcamp, ccMixter, The Hype Machine, imeem, Last.fm, MySpace Music, ReverbNation.com, ShareTheMusic, Soundclick, SoundCloud, Turntable.fm, 8tracks.com*
- **Photography & Art Sharing:** *Instagram, Pinterest, Flickr, Picasa, deviantArt, Photobucket, SmugMug, Zooomr, Webshots*

- **Presentation Sharing:** *Prezi, scribd, SlideShare*

- **Video Sharing:** *YouTube, Qik, Vimeo, Dailymotion, Metacafe, Nico Nico Douga, Openfilm, sevenload, Viddler*

Reviews & Opinions

- **Business Reviews:** *Customer Lobby, Yelp, Inc.*

- **Community Q&A:** *ask.com, Askville, EHow, Quora, Stack Exchange, WikiAnswers, Yahoo! Answers*

- **Product Reviews:** *epinions.com, MouthShut.com, Yelp.com, Cnet.com, Amazon.com*

Many of these applications began as consumer toys. Many evolved into bona fide consumer applications. Now they're migrating into businesses of all kinds. This is "consumerization" – *and pragmatism* – at work. The evolution and direction of social media applications is important to understanding its potential – especially when software applications originate in fun/play mode versus work mode. The ability of "fun" applications to penetrate personal spaces is high – always has been – whereas the ability of "work" applications to penetrate "fun" ones is low – always has been. The assumption that one can find friends in real-time, for example, can – if properly nurtured – extend to assumptions about the location and preferences of customers. The sharing of information with friends of like-minds can extend to the sharing of information with employees, partners and, of course, customers. "Discussions," "arguments" and "negotiations" can also extend beyond the strict confines of personal networks. Applications like virtual reality-based simulations and really simple syndication (RSS) – among others – illustrate how intuitive extensions really are. Companies now proudly exist in Second Life (www.secondlife.com) and CRM processes now include social filters for their clients.

But perhaps the most important extension is "listening." Just as individuals want to know what their "friends" are saying about them, so too do companies need to know what their employees, partners, suppliers and customers are saying about them and their competitors. This can all be measured with social media listening and the "sentiment" that listening reveals. Suffice it to say here that the collection and interpretation of social media data can provide invaluable analyses and insight to companies who want to know what everyone says and thinks about them – and – most importantly – how that affects what they do.

This has always been the Holy Grail: *tell me what my customers really think about me and how – and why – they're likely to buy more or less of what I'm selling based on what they believe and how they feel.* Marketing and branding professionals take this data and re-craft their messages to consumers whose social media interactions profile their values, beliefs and attitudes about companies, products and services.

The previous list of social media applications is a smorgasbord of applications waiting to go to work. The savvy social media strategist takes all of these applications and matches them to short- and longer-term business requirements. While many of them will fall right through the relevance cracks, some will rise to the top as hugely powerful processes and solutions to some difficult problems.

What should you do with all of these applications (and the data they generate)?

A good social media strategy begins with business requirements and ends with the optimal matching of those requirements with alternative social media processes, behaviors and applications. The opportunity lies in the identification of the business processes, activities and models that might be cost-effectively enabled and improved by social media.

Social Media @ Work

Your social media strategy should match business requirements with technology applications within the context of expected value. The business requirements should be defined around business processes and models that enable cost savings, revenue generation, improved service and/or regulatory compliance. The strategy should yield a slate of projects likely to achieve specific objectives.

Let's look at several application areas in some detail. The six areas are defined around five questions, though the five by no means represent all of the questions social media can answer.

Market Research

What are the market research questions social media can answer?

Here's a sampling:

- What are the product & service trends in my industry?

- Where does my company stand in the marketplace?

- What does the competitive landscape look like?

- What are the major regulatory issues I face?

- What do people love/hate about my industry?

Brand & Marketing Intelligence

What are the brand and marketing intelligence questions social media can help answer?

Here's a sampling:

- What are they saying about our products & services?

- What products do they love/hate? Why?

- What are they saying about our company?

- Has sentiment changed over time?

- Why do customers buy from us?

Competitive Intelligence

What are the competitive intelligence questions social media can answer?

Here's a sampling:

- Who are our major and minor competitors?

- What are our customers saying about them?

- What are they saying about us?

- Who are we compared to?

- Who's number 1? Why?

Product Innovation & Life Cycle Management

What are the product innovation and life cycle management questions social media can answer?

Here's a sampling:

- Which new products have excited our customers?

- Which features work for them? Which do not?

- Which features should we introduce first?

- What new products do our customers want?

- Which do they hate?

Customer Service

What are the customer service questions social media can answer?

Here's a sampling:

- What do our customers like about our customer service?

- What services do they like the least?

- What are the "standard" complaints about our service?

- What are customer service "best practices"?

- What do people like most about our competitors customer service?

Threat Assessment

In the defense world, there's something called "Indications & Warnings" – "I&W" for short. Billions and billions of tax dollars are spent on I&W. The idea is simple: everyone wants to know what's going to happen, especially the bad things. So governments watch and worry. They use satellites, spies and even count the number of pizzas delivered late at night to their I&W counterparts (really).

So what about companies?

- What complaints are appearing over and over again?

- What are "Moms" threatening to do to us?

- What are the greatest threats we face?

- What will the government do next?

- What crises are likely to explode?

Social Media Strategy

There's no question that SBI is a priority. Without SBI how can anyone know what their customers think, who they like and who they hate? But there's much more to social media than meets the eye. Understanding the nature and trajectory of the social cloud is huge. It also enables additional primary and secondary business analyses. For example, the entertainment industry's social media intelligence might well focus on what people are saying about specific movies, television programs and radio spots. Tweets, posts and blog entries can add depth and color to commentary on various entertainment venues, but they can also provide additional insights into viewer/listener involvement and from that, infer which content is the most valuable to artists and advertisers, among other target groups.

Social media can help correlate viewer/listener involvement with all sorts of activities through the gathering and analysis of social media intelligence. This kind of analysis can revolutionize the way we think about entertainment ratings, which will evolve from "what did you watch at 10PM" to "how involved were you in what you watched at 10PM" based on your participation in social media before, during and after your viewing of/listening to the content. Social media can also help design, test and deploy products and product enhancements. Why in the world would a company believe it absolutely knows what its customers want? Why not ask them? Why not try before you build – via social media?

Social media is tailor-made for innovation. Why not ask anyone and everyone about what's new? Open innovation is based on social media: ask and you shall receive.

How about competitive intelligence? Just listen to what they're saying about you and the competition. Listen to what they like and hate about you and your competitors. Listen to what they're saying about your competition's customer service.

The whole world of threat tracking and crisis management is huge. How many companies drive themselves into a ditch? Just about all of them at one time or another. How deep is the ditch? What's the best way to get out?

What about politics? What constituents say about their representatives – as sorry as most of them are – is of enormous value to politicians. Social media might actually become a communications channel that politicians can never turn off. It has already become a source of influence.

Last but not least, there are whole movements affected by social media. Who can deny the impact that social media's had on global political events like what we've seen in Egypt, Iran and Syria. It's positively amazing the power that Facebook and Twitter demonstrated in those countries. Are national and global referenda far behind?

Social, Social, All the Time

Why is social so compelling?

There are five characteristics we should understand:

The first is **reach**: As of this writing (2013), Facebook has more than 1,000,000,000 users and Twitter has over 500,000,000. Over 1,000,000,000 use YouTube monthly. Facebook is still growing, and Twitter is growing even faster. In addition to these platforms are thousands of others that have specific missions (like travel, sports, politics, health, etc.). These platforms are also growing dramatically: everyone likes to talk; everyone has an opinion.

According to Neal O'Farrell (way back in 2011), "In The Headlines: Exactly How Big Is Facebook?," September 6, 2011"

> *"More than 250 million of Facebook users access Facebook through their mobile devices. 50% of active Facebook users log in on any given day. The average Facebook user has 130 friends, is connected to 80 community pages, groups and events, and creates 90 pieces of content each month. People around the world spend over 700 billion combined minutes on Facebook pages every month. And exactly what are all these people doing on Facebook? Viewing more than 900 million pages, groups, events, and community pages. Or browsing through more than 30 billion Web links, news stories, blog posts, notes, photo albums and other content. And they're probably using the more than 20 million applications installed every day on Facebook, created by an army of entrepreneurs in more than 190 countries."*

The second characteristic is **credibility**: we know that just about everyone believes what their friends tell them versus what paid talking heads tell anyone. While social media is full of strange and inaccurate tweets, blogs and posts, it's also full of honest insight and thoughts. After decades of "false advertising" and very little regulation around what advertiser's say or do, the perfect storm has created a communications and collaboration channel that's also unregulated – *but perceived as much more credible.*

12

The third is **ubiquity and pervasiveness**: the stage is set for continuous listening – and the analysis of what we hear. We've never had such access to customers, suppliers, employees, partners and competitors. "Release-and-listen" is the new product/service development strategy. "Listen-or-die" is the new customer service mantra.

The fourth characteristic is **volume**: where no one would want to develop a corporate strategy based on a few posts on a few social media sites, when there are thousands of posts a week on major (and minor) brands, products and services, it's easy to infer sentiment (and more) and trajectory and then craft reactive and proactive responses. As volume grows – which it inevitably will – more and more use will be made of social media data, since volume statistically validates the inferences and conclusions companies require regarding their products and services.

The fifth is **demographics**: while social media has been embraced by all age groups, generations X and Y are major participants and will continue to be so throughout their lives. (Generation Z will not differentiate social media from media of any kind and will seamlessly integrate social media-based communication and collaboration into their personal and professional lives.) *Put another way, the future is about social media, just as the past was about email and transactional corporate Web sites.*

Social media should work with structured data about customers, sales, manufacturing and service by providing insights, explanations and prescriptions: social media optimizes business intelligence (BI) investments. Social media is about integrating unstructured with structured data about products, customers, service, brand management, innovation and all things that touch every aspect of your physical and digital supply chain.

Lest there be any doubt about the pervasiveness of social media, note the following (from Wikipedia as of 2012):

- Social networking now accounts for 22% of all time spent online in the US

- A total of 234 million people age 13 and older in the U.S. used mobile devices in December 2009

- Twitter processed more than one billion tweets in December 2009 and averages almost 40 million tweets per day

- Over 25% of U.S. Internet page views occurred at one of the top social networking sites in December 2009, up from 13.8% a year before

- Australia has some of the highest social media usage in the world: in usage of Facebook, Australia ranks highest, with over nine million users spending almost nine hours per month on the site

- The number of social media users age 65 and older grew 100 percent throughout 2010, so that one in four people in that age group are now part of a social networking site

- As of May 2012 Facebook has 901 million users

- Social media has overtaken pornography as the # 1 activity on the Web

- In June 2011, it was reported that iPhone applications hit one billion in nine months, and Facebook added 100 million users in less than nine months

- If Facebook were a country it would be the world's third largest in terms of population, larger even than the US.

- In June 2011, it was also reported that a U.S. Department of Education study revealed that online students outperformed those receiving face-to-face instruction

- YouTube is the second largest search engine in the world

- In four minutes and 26 seconds 100+ hours of video will be uploaded to YouTube

- One out of eight couples married in the U.S. last year met via social media according to statistics released June 2011

- One in six higher education students are enrolled in an online curriculum

- In November 2011, it was reported Indians spend more time on social media than on any other activity on the Internet

- According to a report by Nielsen, "In the U.S. alone, total minutes spent on social networking sites has increased 83 percent year-over-year: in fact, total minutes spent on Facebook increased nearly 700 percent year-over-year, growing from 1.7 billion minutes in April 2008 to 13.9 billion in April 2009, making it the # 1 social networking site for the month"

Social Media Due Diligence

Social business intelligence is not just about listening to Twitter. It's not about listening to the nice things being said about your company. It's not locating social media listening in a business silo. There is governance around social media and SBI. There are also technology and acquisition issues, like whether a company should build an in-house SBI capability or whether it should find a partner that listens and analyzes on behalf of the company. In fact, there are many issues, opportunities and risks associated with SBI. Let's look at ten of the most critical to optimizing SBI.

1. All Social Data Is Not Created Equal

The sheer volume of social media data scares even the most capable database manager. So many companies and their social media listening partners *only sample social media data streams* with (sometimes small) subsets of posts, tweets and blogs used to (only) profile sentiment, customer service and brands.

Not everyone is aware that social media data is frequently purchased by social media listening companies. The listening companies do this because collecting/filtering/structuring social media data is not their core competency (even though they are social media listening companies!). They also do this because even if they could collect all of the data they need to fulfill client requirements, the cost of doing so is often too high for them to remain profitable – so they sample rather than collect all social media data.

They also search social media sites awkwardly, usually with only client-provided keywords that are difficult if not impossible to separate from "noise." The proverbial signal-to-noise problem is huge – and growing – with social media data. The vast majority of posts, tweets and blogs are of little or no use to specific company needs. It's therefore important to find the right signals. But doing so requires a social media collection/filtering/structuring capability that very few social media listening companies actually have – in spite of what they might tell their clients.

Managers and executives should also understand that most social media listening companies get only partial feeds from sites like Twitter and Facebook and don't go deep into the Web to collect the hard-to-find communities and industry-related websites relevant to their clients' businesses. This is because most of the most relevant websites are extremely difficult to penetrate for social data collection and because they don't have simple RSS filters (really simple syndication) and API (application programming interface) feeds. So the social media listening companies just don't hear them. This is a major data collection problem.

Another "all-data's-not-created-equal" issue is data filtering. Most keyword-based social media tools do not take natural language processing, semantic analysis, concept clustering and context into consideration. Charts and graphs are important, but only when they represent data that's meaningful. Social media data analysis should yield clear influence hierarchies, that is, insights into who the most influential authors/publishers are – and are not. It should also be possible to identify gender, location, political affiliation and other profile characteristics from tweets, blogs and posts. A robust social media collection/filtering/structuring engine will embellish the data with verifiable extensions that add richness to the analyses that everyone wants to perform.

Finally, it should be possible to not only collect all of the data your clients need, categorize it, enhance it *and* structure it, but also prepare it for additional use in enterprise CRM, BI and data base management (DBM) platforms. This last capability is essential to extending the power of social media data and integrating it into the processes and software applications that so many companies have deployed. (This is discussed in more detail below).

So what should a social media listening company be able to do with data? Here's a representative list of basic capabilities:

- Data Processing: the set of machines, processor cores, memory, storage capacity and network bisection bandwidth composing the platform that executes all processes.

- Data Harvesting: refers to the mechanisms used to gather data from social networks, forums, blogs, and the Web in general. The mechanisms include paid data aggregation services, source-defined APIs (application programming interfaces), and site-specific scrapers, among other collection techniques.

- Data Storage: refers to a scalable storage system, normally in the form of a database management system (DBMS) and hard (or solid-state) disks attached to the physical machines via different types of links, with different levels of bandwidth and latency.

- Data Filtering: lexical and semantic adaptive filters dedicated to sifting through a global Internet fire-hose, letting through only those items that are relevant to a specific topic. Topics can be extremely narrow or extremely broad.

- Data Indexing: scalable global data search indexes used for old data analysis. These indexes should be global or topic-specific.

- Data Analysis: enables the analysis of all collected filtered data to answer the questions associate with a topic.

- Data Delivery: delivers data and the results of the data analysis.

- Interactive Research: allows humans monitoring a topic to do more in-depth data analysis through the execution of queries or feedback into the learning engines of the data analysis system.

- When all is said and done, a social media listening company should be able to:

- Collect 100's of millions of data snippets daily

- Classify, index and store 100's of millions of items/day in real time, with average latency times of 40 milliseconds

- Use lexical, semantic and statistical filters

- Use machine learning techniques to continuously improve data filters

- Extract author and publisher information; harvest demographics and augment demographics through the use of statistical models and machine learning techniques

- Use supercomputing, multi-level systolic pipelines and map-reduce (beyond the capabilities of Hadoop), cloud resource scheduling, process migration, 1000's of CPU's, terabytes of memory and petabytes of storage

These capabilities permit the collection, filtering, analysis and structuring of deep, relevant social media data.

Without these capabilities, procuring companies will travel an expensive path to modest results.

2. Social Data Must Integrate

Integration and interoperability are always on the short list of capabilities that technologists and savvy managers require. Managers define integration around processes, while technologists define it around their technology hardware platforms, software applications and databases. In order for integration to be effective, it must satisfy both definitions.

Processes around customer service, for example, are traditionally defined around client services, conflict resolution and larger supply chain efficiencies, which means that social process integration needs to occur within existing functions, such as CRM, brand management, customer service, innovation and crisis management. These are only some of the functions impacted by social media. In CRM, for example, social customer relationship management (SCRM) assumes the collection, analysis and inspection of social media data. It assumes that social media data is used to add depth to the analysis of customer relationships, to add explanatory power around why customers buy more – or less – and yield to up-selling and cross-selling opportunities.

In order for social media data to be impactful, the analytical processes around key functions must be modified to include social data. This requires process changes *and* process governance. Companies that fail to modify their functional processes and the governance that supports them will fail to integrate social media into their operating models.

On the technology side, things are more complicated. Note that process always precedes technology so technology integration should stand on the shoulders of process integration. That said, for social media data to be impactful it must integrate into the primary analytical and transactional platforms that medium and large enterprises have deployed, platforms such as CRM, BI, statistical analysis, ERP and DBM, and others that power so many companies. This means that social media data should feed these platforms and integrate into the analytical processes the platforms support.

This is no easy feat. Enterprise platforms are notoriously fickle when it comes to integration: proprietary software applications seldom cooperate with one another. Social media listening companies need to understand the structures and processes of numerous software applications – after they structure all of the unstructured social data they collect and filter. In the trenches this means that structured social media data must integrate with at least the major platforms such as those from IBM, Oracle, SAP, SAS and Microsoft. Within these vendors' worlds are various CRM, BI, statistical analysis, ERP and DBM platforms each with their own unique technology and process integration requirements. Social media teams must be able to feed these platforms as though social media data was made to seamlessly integrate into their technology and functional operating models.

A capable social media listening team should therefore be able to perform the following integration tasks:

- Define social process definitions across major corporate functional areas

- Structure filtered social media data

- Integrate structured/filtered social media data into enterprise platforms such as CRM, BI, statistical and DBM software applications represented by the major technology vendors

3. Social Media Can Be Modeled

Social media data is sometimes perceived as random, disjointed and inconsistent chatter about brands, products and services. One of the myths about social media is that it's only for kids who like to announce their presence at their favorite bars, for chronic complainers and for grandparents connecting with their kids and grandkids. In fact, social media data can reveal much more about what customers, employees and suppliers think, believe and feel: social media data – when expertly modeled – can yield explanatory and predictive insight that otherwise would simply fall between the analytical cracks of keyword-based social media listening.

What can be modeled?

Can social media, for example, reveal insight into the state of a company's "wellness"? Can a diagnostic set of social media indicators of corporate wellness (growth and decline) be identified and validated? Can traditional empirical corporate performance metrics be integrated with social media indicators to build comprehensive predictive models of corporate wellness? Can specific wellness outcomes be correlated with social media? Can Twitter feeds predict behavior, such as box-office receipts, new product success and the next fad?

Examples of social media posts that would indicate corporate health – or illness – include (positive or negative) references to the senior management team, the failure (or success) of new products, audit problems, revenue projections, quality problems, office closings, layoffs, hiring, new store openings, and bill collection notices, among countless others. The modeling challenge is to identify the combinations of indicators that reveal predictive patterns.

Tweets have already been used to measure movie sentiment and box-office revenue with amazing accuracy. Note the work of Asur and Bernardo who predicted the movie "Dear John" would earn $30.71 million at the box office on its opening weekend. It actually generated $30.46 million. For the movie "The Crazies," they predicted a $16.8 million opening: it generated $16.07 million. According to the authors of the National Science Foundation (NSF)-supported study,

> *"We use the chatter from Twitter.com to forecast box-office revenues for movies. We show that a simple model built from the rate at which tweets are created about particular topics can outperform market-based predictors. We further demonstrate how sentiments extracted from Twitter can be further utilized to improve the forecasting power of social media."* (See Sitaram Asur and Bernardo A. Huberman, *Predicting the Future With Social Media*, Web Intelligence and Intelligent Agent Technology (WIIAT), 2010 IEEE/WIC /ACM International Conference Social Computing Lab., HP Labs., Palo Alto, CA, USA, August 31, 2010-September 3, 2010 for more information on social media modeling. Also see www.hpl.hp.com/research/scl/papers/socialmedia)

Social media can predict a wide range of events and behaviors. The military is looking at social media for I&W, the early prediction of unpleasant global events. Companies are using social media to predict if a new sneaker will soar – or crash – and analysts are tapping into social media blogs, tweets and posts to determine the timing and nature of whole social movements. As we've seen, who can deny the impact that social media has had on global political events in Iran, Egypt, Libya and Wall Street? The global "Occupy" movement is another example of just how powerful – and predictive – social media is.

What about electoral politics? What constituents say about their representatives is of enormous value – and risk – to politicians. Social media has become a communications channel that politicians cannot control, but can influence. "Social models" are under development that are initially proving to be every bit as predictive as proverbial survey and focus group data. Note the results of early research of Andranik Tumasjan, Timm O. Sprenger, Philopp G. Sandner and Isabel M. Welpe, "Predicting Elections with Twitter," International Conference on WebLogs & Social Media, Washington, DC, USA, May 25, 2010 for additional information on election modeling; also see "Can Social Media Predict the Election Results?,"http://www.prweb.com/releases/2010/10/prweb4641374.h tm, New York, NY (PRWEB) October 13, 2010. Also see: http://www.electionarena.com:

"In the Senate Primary Races, winners of 8 of the 10 contested Senate primary races were predicted by the number of Facebook supporters the candidates had a week before the elections. Similarly, in the Congressional Primary Races, winners of 42 of the 57 contested Congressional primary races were predicted by the number of Facebook supporters. Are these findings indicative? Campaigning on the internet and social media has been widely discussed as a potential catalyst for grassroots action and social change. As a prediction tool, future studies will tell whether online social networks can act as a proxy for predicting election results. As **The Economist** *noted, the power of traditional polls in predicting election results has been declining since fewer Americans have landline phones, making the population samples pollsters use more and more prone to statistical biases."*

The end-game is the identification, combination and validation of social indicators predictive of specific events, behaviors and conditions. Ideally, these "soft" indicators are combined with more traditional empirical indicators to develop robust predictive models that can explain and forecast a variety of events, behaviors and conditions.

Social media teams should have the ability to do the following:

- Identify diagnostic behavioral indicators

- Develop explanatory and predictive models across industries

- Validate adaptive explanatory and predictive models

Listening teams without these capabilities can only provide limited interpretations of what they hear.

4. Derivative Analytics

The world is awash in predictive analytics (PA) vendors, white papers and case studies. PA has always been about predicting what, where and when – regardless of the domain. BI is actually now a subset of PA – not the other way around as it conceptually should be. But there's another dimension to BI/PI that social media data enables: derivative analytics (DA). While there's always a reluctance to crown yet another analytical area – especially when we're still not too sure where BI ends and PA begins – social media provides a first, second, third and Nth-order context to feelings, beliefs and behavior. Understanding the nature and trajectory of the social crowd is huge, which enables additional primary, secondary and Nth-order analyses.

Here's an example of DA. If you listen to what readers of *Cosmopolitan Magazine* are saying about the magazine you will quickly learn what they like and don't like, what articles they find most useful and the clothes they absolutely must buy. The cover of "Cosmo" is always the subject of blogs, tweets and posts – especially if it has a celebrity sporting a special outfit (which it usually does). But if you listen closely, you can infer much more than what's literally being said. It's possible to profile the conversationalists by gender (almost all are female), age, physical location, time of day, race, religious orientation, influence and other variables that together describe the total conversational context, which is what enables DA. In the case of Cosmo readers, it's possible to know exactly what they're doing when they read the magazine. They might be drinking tea, polishing their nails, shaving their legs, talking to their mothers, Facetiming their friends, texting, or eating pizza. What if a preponderance of readers were doing many of the same things and what if *Cosmo* only advertised in a few of the active areas? Social evidence that, for example, 22% of all *Cosmo* readers read in bed while drinking tea provides an immediate opportunity for tea vendors of all kinds to showcase their wares to an audience predisposed to what they're selling. Showcasing could be directly in the magazine, on the *Cosmo* web site, and through *Cosmo* tweets, blogs and posts to their fans about all of the tea merchandise they might purchase. For this empirical targeted audience – validated by DA – *Cosmo* could charge its advertisers more than it now does.

Similarly, the entertainment industry's DA might focus on what people are saying about specific movies, television programs, commercials, concerts and radio spots. Tweets, posts and blog entries can add depth and color to commentary on various entertainment venues, but they can also provide additional insights into viewer/listener involvement and from those inferences, which content is the most valuable to artists and advertisers, among other target groups. Social media can help correlate viewer/listener involvement with all sorts of activity through the gathering and analysis of social media intelligence. This kind of analysis can revolutionize the way we think about entertainment ratings, which will evolve from "what did you watch at 10PM" to "how involved were you in what you watched at 10PM" based on your participation in social media before, during and after your viewing of/listening to specific content.

What someone says, what someone means and what someone does in the context of a literal post, tweet or blog is the essence of DA. Maps that describe and follow conversations reveal opportunities and risks for companies, brand managers and marketers looking to mine social media data as widely and deeply as possible. DA is discover-able, not predictably model-able. But patterns can be observed and defined as they emerge. They also repeat themselves. While it's impossible to predict that movie goers will – after watching the opening scene of a film about restaurants – become hungry for Crème Brulee, it is possible to observe it – and respond for a variety of business purposes.

The key is context. The wider and deeper the social context in which the data is interpreted the more inferences can be made. Since social conversations are by nature multi-dimensional – with multiple simultaneous conversations occurring continuously – there are numerous ways to parse conversational trajectories, content and purposes. We've learned that a Web site where new babies are discussed is also the site where weight loss and part-time work is discussed. The trick is to understand that what passes as focused discussion on one site is actually opportunistically unfocused since there are no rules about what can or cannot be posted, tweeted or blogged. The ability to travel down these endless conversational paths and extract meaning and purpose is a core competency of the best social media listening companies. Unfortunately, many listening companies do not have the ability to conduct DA.

Social media vendors should have the following DA abilities:

- Track, parse and profile multiple conversations simultaneously

- Contextualize conversations well beyond initial or trigger content and discussions

- Infer from multiple levels of analysis

These capabilities are critical to extending the diagnostic usefulness of SBI.

5. Social Media is Internal, External, Active & Passive

Much of the focus of social media is external – on what customers are saying and what competitors are doing. But lots of social media occurs within companies among their employees, suppliers and partners. It's important to remember that social media includes all stakeholders, all the time.

We also tend to think more about social media listening than social media engagement. In fact, one of the primary reasons to listen is to reactively and pro-actively engage stakeholders.

Figure 1 presents the matrix that, in turns, suggests where social media investments should be made. A comprehensive social media strategy acknowledges the importance of all four cells in the matrix. All cells in the matrix are created equal – in spite of most of the emphasis placed on external versus internal and listening versus engagement. Employee demographics require companies to not only listen to their employees but to enable their social preferences by providing social technology and processes that encourage social media-based communication and collaboration. Suppliers and partners also require social media capabilities – and all of the internal social activity should be ananlyzed across all sorts of behavior and performance metrics.

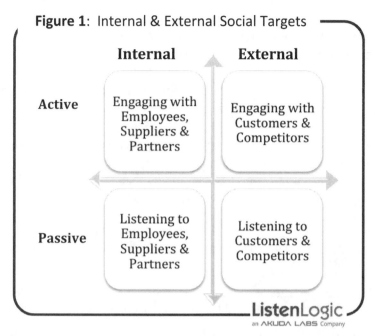

Figure 1: Internal & External Social Targets

	Internal	**External**
Active	Engaging with Employees, Suppliers & Partners	Engaging with Customers & Competitors
Passive	Listening to Employees, Suppliers & Partners	Listening to Customers & Competitors

ListenLogic
an AKUDA LABS Company

The external listening imperative is clear and companies have embraced the need to listen to their customers and competitors. The engagement challenge is more complicated, especially since it depends on the quality of listening data collected, filtered, classified and analyzed.

Engagement requires an approach that is – like customer service – focused on relationship-building. When a customer applauds or complains about a product or service, what should the response be? How should a response be structured? What "if-then" rules should apply? For example, if a customer complains three times about an experience with a company – and that customer is wealthy and socially influential – how, when and in what form should that customer be engaged? Put another way, engagement is much more complicated than posting coupons on Groupon. In fact, engagement runs the gamut of proactive and reactive approaches to SBI. Among other things, social media can help design, test and deploy products and product enhancements.

Why would a company believe it absolutely knows what its customers want? Why not ask them – via social media – along an engagement continuum? Why not try before they build – via social media? Innovation is also a proactive opportunity. Why not ask anyone and everyone about what's new? Open innovation is, in fact, based on social media crowdsourcing.

Listening is unfulfilled social media; engagement converts listening into strategies and tactics. Both listening and engagement are internal and external pastimes. Social media teams should have the following internal/external/active/passive abilities:

- Segment social media activities and targets with appropriate business processes and technologies that optimize listening and engagement opportunities

- Develop suites of internal/external/active/passive strategies and tactics designed to find the right listening and engagement combinations

- Pilot alternative listening/engagement opportunities, especially in areas that exploit the collaboration/connectivity strengths of social media, like crowdsourcing

These capabilities are essential to developing holistic listening-to-analysis-to-engagement approaches to SBI.

6. Real-Time Versus Old-Time

Some events and processes require real-time listening and response. The whole world of threat tracking and crisis management is one of the most significant real-time areas. As already mentioned, how many companies drive themselves into a ditch? Just about all of them at one time or another. How deep is the ditch? What's the best way to get out of it? Is it getting bigger? These are just a few of the questions that require real-time social media.

Definitions are important when discussing real-time, near-real-time and slow(er)-time. Real-time is *real-time*: immediate, with extremely low latency. Near-real-time often refers to response times that are delayed by some measurable increment that can range from minutes to hours or even days. Responses that are weeks old are not near-real-time. Slower-time reporting can range from days to months.

Real-time listening is essential for a range of activities, behaviors and events that create corporate risk – or unique opportunities. Threat analysis is an obvious example of the need for real-time listening. Certain financial events also require real-time listening and engagement. Real-time is useful when action, reaction and engagement are immediately required to mitigate some event or condition, or to capitalize on some special opportunity.

While some real-time requirements are easy to understand, others are not. Financial events often require real-time reporting as do the announcements and initiatives of key competitors.

Management must decide about the need for real-time SBI by taking the following steps:

- Identify the events, behaviors and conditions that qualify as real-time targets

- Build or buy a real-time listening/engagement capability

- Develop "what-if"/"if-then" scenarios for real-time listening/engagement

7. Man Versus Machine

This is a perennial issue, especially as expectations about automation grow. The allocation of tasks across analysts and algorithms is a moving target, since automation technologies continue to improve. The old arguments about what machines can and cannot do rage on. Some believe that there are tasks that only humans can perform; others believe that it's only a matter of time before even the most complex tasks – like flying and landing aircraft – are completely automated.

Social media is complicated and requires two-dimensional domain depth. The first refers to the language and "conversation" of social media, while the second refers to the domains to which social media applies. There are countless words, phrases and abbreviations, among other language artifacts, that enable social media conversations. While many of these artifacts can be interpreted by smart machines, others are not so easily deciphered.

The vertical domains in which social media occurs are also complicated. There are whole lexicons (different from the social media language and communications artifacts) for vertical business domains that require an understanding of the domains that's difficult to comprehensively code in a software application – regardless of how "intelligent" it might be. The retail, pharmaceutical, manufacturing, financial services, insurance, entertainment and chemical industries, among others, have unique processes, histories, best practices, trajectories, cost models and even customer service protocols – among other differences – that require an understanding that machines can interpret at a deductive level but never at an inductive one. We are still some years away from comprehensive vertical knowledge representation so it's necessary to augment whatever artificial intelligence that exists with targeted organic intelligence.

All of this means that there's a necessary social media partnership between man and machine. It's impossible – for now, at least – to expect machines to have deductive and inductive knowledge about every vertical industry, or for machines to comprehend and interpret every language artifact for all social conversationalists – especially since they change all the time. Human analysts are a necessary part of the SBI process. Note that this is no different from what governments have acknowledged for years as they listen to what their global competitors are doing. Their "I&W" operations have relied on both men and machines to forecast global events for decades. While the machines get smarter and smarter, there's no substitute for the insight and analysis that subject matter experts (SMEs) can provide.

Perhaps the riskiest social media listening practice is keyword-based listening, where keywords are expected to yield the most insightful analysis without deep contextual domain or social language understanding. Machines may be good at finding keywords from sampled social media data streams, but they're far from perfect at interpreting what the keywords mean or using keyword-based listening to engage customers or predict events. Better collection/filtering/structuring can help a lot, but the more complicated the data the more we need subject matter experts to participate in the whole SBI process.

Social media vendors – or an in-house social media listening/engaging team – should have the ability to do the following:

- Allocate SBI tasks along a man-machine continuum that realistically assigns the right tasks to the right agent

- Recognize – and invest in – a balanced man-machine SBI platform

- Continuously assess the state of SBI automation, especially as it pertains to vertical industry knowledge representation

8. Acquiring Social Business Intelligence

The age-old technology acquisition question applies to social media listening and analysis: build or buy? When Salesforce.com bought the social media listening company Radian6, it announced that social listening would move to the Salesforce.com cloud, where clients could rent a tool that would perform keyword searches whenever and wherever they wanted. Other social media tool companies have the same approach. But some others see social media as more complex, requiring some supporting analysis to fully understand

31

what the social conversations mean especially across very different industries.

There are several social media acquisition options. The first option is classic: build an internal social media listening capability by hiring and training professionals, build/license/acquire social media listening (and analytical) technology, and develop internal processes for leveraging social media across the enterprise.

The second option is consistent with emerging acquisition and deployment best practices, as cloud computing rises in popularity and improves its capabilities. More and more companies are renting listening and engagement technologies and expertise rather than building those capabilities in-house.

There are also hybrid acquisition models that combine aspects of core competency and urgency decision criteria, among others. Some companies might, for example, purchase large amounts of social media data, hire a vendor to build some interfaces to their CRM platforms, then build an internal analytical capability to optimize SBI. Companies might also hire consultants to build models that their in-house statistical packages might run, or integrate data into their BI platforms.

Many companies today are defaulting to small initial projects that test the value of social media listening and engagement, but the real question is not the build versus buy one, or even the hybrid one. The real question is about expertise and it's optimal location.

Figure 2: Social Media Capabilities & Acquisition Options

Capabilities & Acquisition Options	Data Collection & Filtering	Integration	Modeling	Derivative Analytics	Internal/ External/ Listen/ Engage	Real-Time	Man Versus Machine	Measurement	Social Media Strategy
In-House									
Outsourced									
Hybrid									

ListenLogic
an AKUDA LABS Company

The matrix in Figure 2 helps with an acquisition options assessment. Some best practices are emerging that should help companies decide how and what they want to acquire. Best SBI practices also suggest that modeling, derivative analytics (DA), internal/external/listening/ engagement campaigns, man-machine task allocation, measurement and social media strategy be developed in-house. The hybrid areas include modeling, DA, and man-versus-machine task allocation – all as suggested in Figure 3. These three areas could stay in-house or be outsourced.

Management should understand the range of social media skills and capabilities and how they should best acquire them:

- Define core competencies around technology generally and social media specifically

- Identify the specific social media capabilities necessary to deliver SBI

- Develop and implement a sourcing strategy that optimizes core competency and SBI requirements

9. Measurement

Social media investment impact must be measured. Business cases should be developed and vetted across the management team to assure support. Social media impact metrics should fall into at least two broad categories: total cost of ownership (TCO) and return on investment (ROI), and each of these categories should be further delineated.

TCO is a traditional metric that identifies and tracks all costs connected with an initiative. Perhaps the most notorious TCO metric is the annual cost of Blackberry support for each employee ($4,250 annually as famously reported by the Gartner Group). ROI is the business impact metric that assesses costs versus benefit. *TCO is a driver of ROI, but business performance metrics are the essence of ROI calculations.*

Figure 3: Social Media Acquisition Best Practices

Capabilities & Acquisition Options	Data Collection & Filtering	Integration	Modeling	Derivative Analytics	Internal/ External/ Listen/ Engage	Real-Time	Man Versus Machine	Measure-ment	Social Media Strategy
In-House	●	●	●	●	●			●	●
Outsourced				●		●	●		
Hybrid			■	■			■		

ListenLogic
an AKUDA LABS Company

Social media is not an especially expensive endeavor. When compared to the largest enterprise technology projects – like ERP, CRM, BI or network and systems management projects – social media is downright cheap. Even the most comprehensive TCO models that include everything that a company might spend on social media will not reveal especially large sums of money – unless a company decides, based on its core competency assessment, that it needs a large sophisticated in-house social media listening and engagement capability. If a company outsources significant parts of its SBI initiative, it's TCO will not be high. The larger question centers around ROI.

ROI is about business impact, so the metrics need to address before-and-after effects of investments in social media "presence," like with Facebook and Twitter (and numerous other platforms), and social media engagement, especially with existing and prospective customers. Traditional metrics around sales, customer service, physical and digital visits, etc. will define the impact of social media initiatives.

As with all useful ROI calculations, companies should begin with metrics aligned to their social media investment objectives. In the short run, these objectives speak to simple activities, like the number of "Likes" on a Facebook page, but longer-term the metrics should speak to objectives that assume that social media is here to stay and will become a continuous communications and collaboration channel.

- Management should focus on TCO and ROI, as follows:

- Develop a comprehensive social media TCO model

- Develop an aligned (to business objectives and requirements) social media ROI model

Distinguish between short-term and longer-term TCO and ROI metrics and adapt calculations to initial social media initiatives and longer-term continuous listening/engagement requirements as the social media channel inevitably becomes permanent

10. Social Business Intelligence Requires a Strategy

How can a company *not* invest in social media? While we spend billions every year on BI, shouldn't we also spend some money on *social* BI? Companies also spend heavily on innovation, focus groups, competitor intelligence and brand management: social media can add a significant dimension of understanding, analysis and action to all of these activities and more. It's also extremely cost-effective. As suggested above, companies can build their own social media listening/responding teams, or contract with any number of vendors that provide social media listening services at fees ranging from the low thousands to the high tens of thousands a month.

Companies should identify opportunities to leverage social media data, information and knowledge by focusing on internal and external processes, functions and objectives. Internal opportunities leverage the same tools companies can use for external SBI. The key is to identify the social media tools likely to have the most impact on a set of internal and external activities that will generate measurable business value.

External activities include listening-for-purpose and more specific activities include market research, brand and marketing intelligence, competitive intelligence, product innovation and life cycle management, customer service, customer relationship management, innovation, reputation management and threat tracking, among other areas. Internal activities include listening to and engaging with employees, suppliers and partners.

Companies should develop strategies that will define their objectives and the means to achieve them:

- Identify the business objectives and requirements wide and deep enough to support the development of a viable social media investment strategy

- Identify the questions whose answers constitute a strategy

- Adapt the strategy to investment results

Social business intelligence is applicable to a variety of problems. *Social risk intelligence* focuses on quantitative and qualitative risks that companies face all the time. What can social media do for risk analysts? Chapter 2 sets the stage.

Chapter 2 - Social Risk Intelligence

As suggested in Chapter 1, social media strategy should match business requirements with technology applications within the context of expected value. The business requirements should be defined around business processes and models that enable cost savings, revenue generation, improved service, regulatory compliance – *and risk assessment and mitigation.* The strategy should yield a slate of social media projects likely to achieve specific objectives. In this case, the emphasis is on the identification, assessment, mitigation and, ultimately, management of risks, and the role that social media listening/engagement plays in that process. Let's review the business of risk and the processes by which risk is identified, assessed, mitigated and managed, as well as the social risk market. We'll then turn to the role that *social risk intelligence* should play in the overall risk identification, assessment, mitigation and management process.

The Business of Risk

Risk intelligence – the ability to make informed decisions about risks based on historical, current and future views of a business – has become a hot topic for organizations, in particular, the *Fortune*-ranked companies under major pressure to improve shareholder value while demonstrating a commitment to social responsibility. Once associated primarily with financial institutions, Risk Committees are now quite common. Their job is to identify, assess, mitigate and manage all of the risks that threaten every company. Among the risks are cyber risks, physical security risks, financial risks, operational risks and risks associated with a company's business model. The formalization of risk identification/assessment/mitigation/management is very much a 21st century core competency. *Social media* risks are "new" – but growing (look at the range of Aetna's problems we discussed in the Preface). Risk is now a business unto itself and social risk is a growing line of (risk) business.

The Range of Risk

There are a variety of risks, including:

- Cyber risks
- Physical security risks
- Financial risks
- Operational risks
- Business model risks

When referencing *cyber security*, Risk Committees most commonly reference the following:

- Business interruption due to cyber attack on their data centers and networks
- Business interruption due to supplier and/or customer cyber disruptions
- Denial of service attack or virus on the organization's servers
- Theft/loss of the organizations assets/intellectual property
- Infringing others' intellectual property
- Privacy violations/data breach of customer records

When referencing *physical security*, like the vulnerability a foreign manufacturing plant to terrorists or civil wars, there are similar lists.

According to Wikipedia:

"Physical security is primarily concerned with restricting physical access by unauthorized people (commonly interpreted as intruders) to controlled facilities, although there are other considerations and situations in which physical security measures are valuable.

"Security inevitably incurs costs and, in reality, it can never be perfect or complete - in other words, security can reduce but cannot entirely eliminate risks. Given that controls are imperfect, strong physical security applies the

principle of defense in depth using appropriate combinations of overlapping and complementary controls. For instance, physical access controls for protected facilities are generally intended to:

- *Deter potential intruders (e.g. warning signs and perimeter markings)*
- *Distinguish authorized from unauthorized people (e.g. using keycards/ access badges)*
- *Delay, frustrate and ideally prevent intrusion attempts (e.g. strong walls, door locks and safes)*
- *Detect intrusions and monitor/ record intruders (e.g. intruder alarms and CCTV systems)*
- *Trigger appropriate incident responses (e.g. by security guards and police)*

"It is up to security designers, architects and analysts to balance security controls against risks, taking into account the costs of specifying, developing, testing, implementing, using, managing, monitoring and maintaining the controls, along with broader issues such as aesthetics, human rights, health and safety, and societal norms or conventions. Physical access security measures that are appropriate for a high security prison or a military site may be inappropriate in an office, a home or a vehicle, although the principles are similar."

In addition to cyber risk and traditional physical security risks, there are *financial risks* that risk committees and risk managers must address. According to Wikipedia, some of these include:

- *"Financial risk: an umbrella term for multiple types of risk associated with financing, including financial transactions that include company loans in risk of default. Risk is a term often used to imply downside risk, meaning the uncertainty of a return and the potential for financial loss.*

- *"Asset-backed risk: risk that the changes in one or more assets that support an asset-backed security will significantly impact the value of the supported security. Risks include interest rate, term modification and prepayment risk.*

- *"Credit risk: also called default risk, credit risk is the risk associated with a borrower going into default (not making payments as promised). Investor losses include lost principal and interest, decreased cash flow, and increased collection costs. An investor can also assume credit risk through direct or indirect use of leverage.*

For example, an investor may purchase an investment using margin. Or an investment may directly or indirectly use or rely on repo, forward commitment, or derivative instruments.

- *"Investment risk: has been shown to be particularly large and particularly damaging for very large, one-off investment projects, so-called "megaprojects". This is because such projects are especially prone to end up in what has been called the "debt trap," i.e., a situation where – due to cost overruns, schedule delays, etc. – the costs of servicing debt becomes larger than the revenues available to pay interest on and bring down the debt.*

- *"Foreign investment risk: the risk of rapid and extreme changes in value due to smaller markets; differing accounting, reporting, or auditing standards; nationalization, expropriation or confiscatory taxation; economic conflict; or political or diplomatic changes. Valuation, liquidity, and regulatory issues may also add to foreign investment risk.*

- *"Liquidity risk: the risk that a given security or asset cannot be traded quickly enough in the market to prevent a loss (or make the required profit). There are two types of liquidity risk: asset liquidity and funding liquidity*

- *"Market risk: the risk that the value of a portfolio, either an investment portfolio or a trading portfolio, will decrease due to the change in market risk factors. The four standard market risk factors are stock prices, interest rates, foreign exchange rates, and commodity prices*

- *"Equity risk: is risk that stock prices in general (not related to a particular company or industry) or the implied volatility will change*

- *"Interest rate risk: is the risk that interest rates or the implied volatility will change*

- *"Currency risk: is the risk that foreign exchange rates or the implied volatility will change, which affects, for example, the value of an asset held in that currency"*

There are also day-to-day operational, reputational, legal and technology risks that must be identified, assessed, mitigated and managed. There are business model risks as well. Who can forget what happened to Circuit City, Blockbuster, Best Buy and Nokia? Business models are at perpetual risk.

All of these risks are real and – arguably – growing, as business becomes faster and more distributed. Globalization exacerbates all risks. Regulatory trends increase risk. Terrorism increases risk. It's risky out there – to put it mildly.

Risk Management

Risks must be identified, assessed, mitigated and, ultimately, managed. Wikipedia describes risk management as follows:

"Risk management is the identification, assessment, and prioritization of risks (defined in ISO 31000 as the effect of uncertainty on objectives, whether positive or negative) followed by coordinated and economical application of resources to minimize, monitor, and control the probability and/or impact of unfortunate events or to maximize the realization of opportunities. Risks can come from uncertainty in financial markets, project failures (at any phase in design, development, production, or sustainment life-cycles), legal liabilities, credit risk, accidents, natural causes and disasters as well as deliberate attack from an adversary, or events of uncertain or unpredictable root-cause. Several risk management standards have been developed including the Project Management Institute, the National Institute of Standards and Technology, actuarial societies, and ISO standards. Methods, definitions and goals vary widely according to whether the risk management method is in the context of project management, security, engineering, industrial processes, financial portfolios, actuarial assessments, or public health and safety.

"Risk management "consists of the following elements, performed, more or less, in the following order:

- *Identify, characterize threats*
- *Assess the vulnerability of critical assets to specific threats*
- *Determine the risk (i.e. the expected likelihood and consequences of specific types of attacks on specific assets)*
- *Identify ways to reduce those risks*
- *Prioritize risk reduction measures based on a strategy*

- *"The International Organization for Standardization (ISO) identifies the following principles of risk management, stating that risk management should:*
- *Create value – resources expended to mitigate risk should be less than the consequence of inaction, or (as in value engineering), the gain should exceed the pain*
- *Be an integral part of organizational processes*
- *Be part of decision making process*
- *Explicitly address uncertainty and assumptions*
- *Be systematic and structured*
- *Be based on the best available information*
- *Be tailor-able*
- *Take human factors into account*
- *Be transparent and inclusive*
- *Be dynamic, iterative and responsive to change*
- *Be capable of continual improvement and enhancement*
- *Be continually or periodically re-assessed*

"Once risks have been identified, they must then be assessed as to their potential severity of impact (generally a negative impact, such as damage or loss) and to the probability of occurrence. These quantities can be either simple to measure, in the case of the value of a lost building, or impossible to know for sure in the case of the probability of an unlikely event occurring. Therefore, in the assessment process it is critical to make the best educated decisions in order to properly prioritize the implementation of the risk management plan.

"Once risks have been identified and assessed, all techniques to manage the risk fall into one or more of these four major categories:

- *Avoidance (eliminate, withdraw from or not become involved)*
- *Reduction (optimize – mitigate)*
- *Sharing (transfer – outsource or insure)*
- *Retention (accept and budget)*

"Risk management plans should propose applicable and effective security controls for managing the risks. For example, an observed high risk of computer viruses could be mitigated by acquiring and implementing antivirus software. A good risk management plan should contain a schedule for control implementation and responsible persons for those actions.

"According to ISO/IEC 27001, the stage immediately after completion of the risk assessment phase consists of preparing a Risk Treatment Plan, which should document the decisions about how each of the identified risks should be handled. Mitigation of risks often means selection of security controls, which should be documented in a Statement of Applicability, which identifies which particular control objectives and controls from the standard have been selected, and why.

"Implementation follows all of the planned methods for mitigating the effect of the risks. Purchase insurance policies for the risks that have been decided to be transferred to an insurer, avoid all risks that can be avoided without sacrificing the entity's goals, reduce others, and retain the rest."

Social Risk Initiatives

Focused almost exclusively on employee usage and posts made by disgruntled customers, awareness of the *risks around social media* is relatively low. Executives understand that there's risk involved in social media; yet this risk has not been well-defined. Governance structures to monitor compliance and manage risk are still in early stages. Risk committees are often misdirected by references to volume ("our technology scours billions of sources"), the meaning of real-time, the reliance on keyword searches, and analytics driven by select sources or vendors (i.e. *Twitter* and *Facebook*). There's a fundamental understanding of the need to monitor social media for threats, but the importance of *how* and *why* is not always recognized.

Of the organizations touting a comprehensive approach to identifying threats to the business, investments typically include a Governance, Risk and Compliance (GRC) solution, cyber insurance, Social CRM, an "integrated" BI platform capable of managing "big data" and a sophisticated approach for network monitoring and virus protection.

There is significant need for real-time threat intelligence for major corporations based on the recognized need, lack of (effective) solution providers and the extensive amount of time required to implement a comprehensive risk intelligence framework. As implementations drag-on, risk committees understand they are leaving their organizations exposed to reputational loss as well as missed social media-driven opportunities for competitive advantage.

There are several technology markets, vendors and products focusing on Risk Intelligence, Business Intelligence, Social Media Monitoring, Threat Intelligence Research Service, Governance Risk and Compliance, just to name a few. All of these forays into social risk intelligence – as diffuse as they may be – are interested in expanding definitions of risk to include *social* risk. Let's look at the industry structure.

Business Intelligence (BI), Analytics & Corporate Performance

Note the following:

- *According to a Gartner Group (www.gartner.com) report, this is a $10.5 billion market*

- *Driver: companies are investing in software platforms to answer 3 critical performance questions: how are we doing? Why? What should we be doing?*

- *The market is expected to have robust growth in 2012 as BI and Analytics are rated #1 priorities in corporate IT, and new growth is coming from "big data"*

- *The major vendors in this space include: SAP, Oracle, IBM and Microsoft – and all of these vendors have, or are perfecting, social risk offerings*

Threat Intelligence Research Service

A subset of the mature Network Security market and Security Information & Event Management (SIEM), Threat Intelligence (a.k.a. Predictive Security) market is another relevant initiative:

- Market Size: IDC Reports the emerging market is set to grow from $198M in 2009 to $905M by 2014

- Addresses cybercrime, i.e. hacking, network attacks

- Market Drivers: Average cost of security incident $234K (according to the *CSI Computer Crime and Security Survey 2009*)

Governance, Risk & Compliance (GRC)

According to Forrester Research (www.forrester.com), "GRC Software Platform Revenues Will Rise To $1.3 Billion In 2011." Once positioned largely as a compliance necessity and cost of doing business, Risk Management has evolved into Risk Intelligence and is considered to be an important enabler for competitive advantage.

According to an Accenture Global Risk Management Study:

- *98% of respondents said that risk management is a higher priority today than it was two years ago*

- *More than 80% of companies surveyed also consider their risk area to be a key management function that helps them deal with marketplace volatility and organizational complexity*

Chief Risk Officers (CROs) have grown in importance and influence and have helped to drive some of the strategic direction.

- *In 2009, Accenture's Global Risk Management Study, comprised of research conducted among different industries, showed that 33% "of firms had a CRO who owned risk management in the organization"*

- *In just two years, that figure had risen to 45% (figures for financial services firms were even higher with 84% having a CRO on board)*

All of this suggests that the business of risk is growing – and growing rapidly, and that the gap between risk intelligence and social risk intelligence is shrinking, though there's still work necessary to get social risk intelligence into C-level discussions and board rooms.

When Things Go Wrong

But no one doubts that risk is expensive. There are litigation, white collar crime and reputational costs that can be substantial.

- *Among Fortune 500 companies, the estimated total cost of litigation in 2008 was $210 billion*

- *For industries with highest spend: healthcare, insurance, energy/utilities, and tele-communication/high-tech sectors litigation spending is more likely to be more than $10 million*

- *In 2009, the average hourly billing rate for an attorney in a small or midsized practice was $284*

- *Examples: Siemens spent $850 million in fees and expenses to investigate anti-corruption; Daimler had a five-year investigation that cost over $500 million*

According to *Hon. Doug Ose (Ohio), Federal Sentencing Guidelines,* $200B - $565B was lost in one year due to "white collar" crime.

According to *Regulatory Sanctions and Reputational Damage in Financial Markets* (J. Armour, C. Mayer, A. Polo, University of Oxford, March 2011):

"We observe that the penalized firms' stock prices experience statistically significant abnormal losses of approximately nine times the fines and compensation paid. We interpret the fall in equity

market value in excess of mandated payments as the firms' reputational loss."

The report looked at 23 companies worth $6 trillion pre-crisis, including AIG, Arthur Andersen, BP, Northern Rock, Cadbury Schweppes:

- *3 collapsed with significant losses, 3 were rescued by the government*

- *There were common themes: risks were not always reported up to board level, but everyone else knew about them in different parts of the organisation*

- *The report called on companies to revitalise and re-think how they viewed risk management introducing new skills and perspectives*

Board members are becoming increasingly aware of the need to adapt to the social world where listening, disclosure, transparency and engaging is expected. Social media provides a means for connecting with corporate stakeholders. Social media is best utilized in a holistic way (integrated with Business Intelligence and Corporate Strategy): social media is marginalized when kept within a silo.

Social Risk Intelligence

Boards of Directors and other corporate executives, managers and stakeholders can find valuable – and actionable – "social" information if they listen and engage.

Note that Boards in particular are responsible for corporate oversight. This includes monitoring and advising the senior executive team as it develops and implements the corporate strategy. Information gleaned through social media might provide unique and relevant insights into the success of these efforts and supplement the traditional key performance indicators (KPIs) that directors use to evaluate management and the success of implemented programs and strategies. This may include employee satisfaction, customer satisfaction, supplier reputation, product/service failure, and product innovation – areas that are traditionally difficult to measure. Information gathered through social media might alert the board to risks facing the organization by using an outside-in view. Examples of the type of risks include:

- *Operational risk – how exposed the company is to disruption of it its operations*

- *Reputational risk – how protected are the company's brands and corporate reputation*

- *Compliance risk – how effectively the company complies with laws and regulations*

The opportunity to identify risks and threats that may impact the company is significantly improved when 'listening' incorporates the conversations of all associated stakeholders (vendors, employees, consumers, investors, etc.).

Study after study reveals that well over 50% of executives believe that reputational risk associated with social media should be a board room issue – but only around 15% of companies currently have a program in place to capture and analyze social data.

Directors are expected to advise on corporate strategy, the business model and risk management, using their personal experience and expertise coupled with information furnished by the corporations' management team. Unless there are specific issues regarding the trustworthiness of the management, the board is best positioned to review social media analytics when the information is provided to them through management.

Social media introduces a new level of detail and complexity to corporate information gathering and analysis. Why haven't more boards of directors made certain that management has a process in place for collecting, analyzing and responding to social information? Do boards actually know what questions to ask? Can boards distinguish between a "good" system for monitoring social media and a "bad" one?

An important aspect of board responsibility is to monitor organizational reputation. How is this currently done? Should overall sentiment derived from social media sources be a primary input for this analysis? Which social media metrics should be presented and which excluded? Where do the responsibilities of the board end and those of management begin?

Boards are acknowledging (but not always effectively addressing) the following:

- *Monitoring of social media – something worth looking at for future-proof risk management, we must recognise social media as a considerable force and threat, which should not be left solely to the PR function to manage*

- *Firms need to shift to a more business performance approach to risk management rather than aligning it simply with regulatory compliance*

The concept of a dedicated, board-level "risk committee" has become a mandated reality at many financial-related firms.

But the need to listen to social media extends well beyond boards of directors. Those responsible for innovation, customer service, brand management and even employee relations all have vested interests in what people say, feel, recommend and loathe.

Social risk intelligence (SRI) extends within, throughout and outside of corporate firewalls. Listening – and engaging – analyzing – then solving – are all activities enabled by SRI.

Ultimately, SRI bifurcates to include:

- *Risks in response to social media*

- *Risks identified through social media*

But there's also a downside. In fact, there's social media exposure that must be considered, including at least:

- *IP (intellectual property)/sensitive data loss – information strategic to the company could be inappropriately released, e.g.: "My company is working on this cool new project to ... "*

- *Compliance violations – data that violates regulatory/compliance requirements could be communicated, e.g.: "You won't believe who I saw just come into the hospital to have this treatment done ... "*

- *Reputational loss – slanderous remarks and comments from a disgruntled employee could create damaging perceptions, e.g.: "If you work for my company, you will be mistreated and not respected ... "*

- *Financial loss – remarks about company performance could impact stock price and performance, e.g.: "The strategic plan for my company is not going to work, and results are not going to be good ..."*

- *Safety loss – release of information about what someone is doing or where someone is traveling, e.g.: "Our executive team is meeting at Location Z ..."*

- *Personal reputation loss – remarks made by an individual or friends of an individual could be viewed by others, e.g.: "Let me tell you what happened the other night when I was out for dinner with my boss. He/she drank so much that ..."*

Companies need "situational awareness" through alert, mapping and analysis of open-source actionable intelligence – open source intelligence collection capability through a robust open source platform that has the flexibility to change search parameters and geo-locate searches based on breaking events, crises or emerging threats.

Companies also need to rapidly assemble and provide critical open source information and intelligence that will allow companies to vet, identify, and geo-locate breaking events, incidents and emerging threats. Such services must have the capacity to allow companies to retain control of cached and real-time proprietary data; the ability to share it with select partners, and ultimately enhancing coordination, synchronized-awareness and synergy at the operational level.

What about threat-related SRI? The following table identifies the range of threat-related intelligence that companies require and SRI vendors should provide:

Competitor Risks	Environmental Risks	Market Risks	Regulatory Risks	Supply Chain Risks
• New entrants	• Accidents	• Shifting consumer trends	• Taxation / margins	• Supplier Compliance
• Acquisitions / joint ventures	• Natural disasters	• Changing demographics	• Transfer pricing / rules	• Quality standards
• New product launches	• Activists	• Economic changes	• Regulatory changes	• Distribution lobbying / cartels
• Aggressive pricing	• Environmental orgs	• Political risk		• Lack of logistics optimization
• Unfair competitive practices (cartels, lobbying, tax evasion, etc.)	• Social media	• New business models or tech		• Unfair or unethical supplier demands with their suppliers
• Uncompetitive OH structure	• Protectionist policies (taxes, import duties etc.)	• Economic downturn		• Manipulation of bargaining power
• HR profiles	• Nationalization	• Changes in customer preferences		• Theft
• Outsourcing processes	• Emission policy	• Product competition		• Inability to fulfill contracts / liabilities
• Substitute products, obsolete tech	• EU certifications	• Bubble economies		• Counter intelligence
• Counter intelligence	• Waste disposal			• Customer mergers
• Protectionism	• Lack of take-back/recycling			• Customer bankruptcy
• Small local competition	• Sourcing			• Supplier bankruptcy
• Management buyouts				• Price and currency fluctuations
• M&A dynamics				• Value chain changes (revenue shifts)

• Environmental
legislation

• Natural disasters

The best SRI technology will pair with subject-matter experts to provide clients with real-time information regarding incidents and emerging themes relating to risk, reputation, crises and threats.

SRI technology and services should also:

- *Have the ability to clear alert or maintain alert until its final resolution (to be determined by client) – ability to re-open (un-archive cached alerts) should additional content surface*

- *Be able to apply/over-lay information for context i.e. record major weather event related to service outage/outrage*

- *Be able to alert format: sent in template format for consistency – answering who, what, where, when and why. This allows client to immediately ingest time-sensitive information upon receipt*

- *Have the ability to disseminate the threat or incident to other stakeholders without needing describe what it is being sent and why (template speaks for itself)*

- *Have the ability to capture and summarize the efforts taken by clients*

- *Be able to provide alert folders to save and archive past reports. Provide clients the ability to revisit historic reports in support of internal activities/inside knowledge. Provide tracking information each time folder is opened (added risk management for companies)*

- *Have the ability to monitor across languages – collect in the native language of speaker*

- *Have the ability to determine the time-frame for the continuous monitoring once an alert is disseminated*

- *Be able to discover patterns of interest*

- *Be able to predict social attacks (like targeting executives, annual meeting protests)*

- *Be able to detect specific, credible threats to monitor adversarial situations*

- *Be able to identify bad actors (activists, saboteurs) and analyze their movements, their expressed timelines, and potential adverse actions that the client can take*

- *Be able to predict likely developments in a specific situation or future actions taken by bad actors (by conducting, trend, pattern, association, and timeline analysis)*

- *Be able to detect instances of deception in intent or action by bad actors for the explicit purpose of misleading the brand or relevant law enforcement*

- *The ability to develop domain and influencer assessments for the purpose of strategic communications (typically in response to an event or crisis)*

- *The ability to develop pattern-of-life matrices to support strategic planning and risk response*

- *Be able to detect potential threats*

- *Be able to develop threat profiles*

- *The ability to outline possible courses-of-action*

- *Be able to determine timeframe for action by actors*

- *Be able to identify and develop a tactical picture of an event*

- *Be able to develop counter-measures (e.g., advocate mapping)*

These are the broad capabilities that an SRI function should have – regardless if it's provisioned internally or through an SRI vendor.

As the above list suggests, corporate risk officers require the following operational SRI capabilities:

- *Real-time, relevant alerts regarding incidents or threats that pose damage to the company*

- *The ability to share, analyze and understand – anytime, anywhere*
- *Real-time visibility for the Risk Committee*

- *Graphical information, interpreted for relevance*

- *Alerts provided in the context of a Risk Management/Risk Intelligence plan*

- *The ability to import alerts for tracking, mapping, reporting and overall analytics including if/them modeling*

- *The ability to customize social influence based on a company's specific needs*

- *Incident Risk Matrices*

- *Anytime/anywhere access*

- *Executive level snapshots/dashboards*

All of these capabilities are important to an effective SRI process. Without the ability to detect, avoid, mitigate and manage risks, they jeopardize their strategies and tactics. In fact, sometimes the effects are horrific – as Chapter 3 demonstrates all too clearly.

Chapter 3 - 100 Social Media Disasters

The 100 social media disasters in this chapter run the gamut from simple mistatements to massive micalculations of judgment.

As you read through them, note what happened, the impact of the crisis and the lessons learned. Also note the range of problems and the number of vertical industries in which they occurred. The list of crises demonstrates clearly that no one is immune to problems, gaffes and worse.

SOCIAL MEDIA DISASTERS

AVOIDING #FAIL

Rogue Employees Violate Domino's Food (1)

What Happened:

Relevant Media

- On Monday April 13, 2009 Domino's employees, Kristy Hammond and Michael Setzer posted videos on YouTube as they violated numerous health code violations while preparing food inside a Domino's kitchen.
- The video was noticed by a blogger and sent to Domino's spokesperson Tim McIntyre on the evening of April 13th.
- On Monday evening, the Consumerist used details in the video to identify the location of the Domino's in Conover, NC.
- On Tuesday, April 14th, Domino's executives decided not to comment in the hope the issue would die down.
- On Tuesday, the franchise owner brought in health inspectors and fired the two employees immediately.
- By Wednesday the YouTube video had over 1 million YouTube views.
- On Wednesday, Kristy Hammonds apologized to the company saying it was a prank and the food was never actually delivered.
- Later that evening, the YouTube video was removed by Hammonds.

Over **1 million views** on YouTube video

Over **800 comments** in 2 days

~100k views on CEO's YouTube apology

Most Shared Sources:

YouTube Video
CEO's YouTube Apology
NY Times Article
ABC News Article

Rogue Employees Violate Domino's Food (2)

Brand Reaction:

- Domino's decided not to comment on Tuesday, one day after the video was posted.
- The franchise owner fired the employees on Wednesday.
- Wednesday afternoon, Domino's started a Twitter account to address concerns, @dpzinfo.
- Wednesday evening, Domino's CEO posted a YouTube video apologizing for the incident.

Lessons Learned:

- Identifying the video immediately is critical. If necessary, take legal action to remove it so it isn't reproduced, else this video will be online forever.
- The range of response options decreases exponentially the longer the video is online.

Relevant Media

Over **1 million views** on YouTube video

Over **800 comments** in 2 days

~100k views on CEO's YouTube apology

Most Shared Sources:

YouTube Video
CEO's YouTube Apology
NY Times Article
ABC News Article

Papa John's Racist Receipt (1)

What Happened:

- On January 7, 2012 Minhee Cho tweeted a picture of a receipt from Papa John's that had her name listed as "lady chinky eyes."
- The tweet included Papa John's Twitter username (@PapaJohns) placing it onto the company's Twitter stream.
- In less than 3 hours, the tweet was reposted hundreds of times and viewed thousands more.
- The assistant manager was unaware of the incident when contacted by *The Huffington Post* that same afternoon.
- The assistant manager said there was no way to identify the employee based on the receipt but said disciplinary action would be taken.

Relevant Media

Over 11,000 retweets and 260,000 views

Papa John's Facebook Post: "We were extremely concerned to learn of the receipt issue in New York. This act goes against our company values, and we've confirmed with the franchisee that this matter was addressed immediately and that the employee is being terminated. We are truly sorry for this customer's experience."

Most Shared Sources:

Minhee Cho Twitpic
Papa John's Facebook Response
Huffington Post Article

Papa John's Racist Receipt (2)

Brand Reaction:

- The assistant manager was unaware on the day of the incident.
- Papa Johns issued a formal apology on Facebook the day of the incident.
- They also posted an abbreviated version on their Twitter account: *"We have issued an apology, are reaching out to customer & franchise employee is being terminated."*

Lessons Learned:

- Tweeting at a specific brand or person typically increases the posts reach significantly (in this case @PapaJohns had ~59,000 Twitter followers).
- Apologizing on Facebook engages an entirely new group of social media users with the issue (in this case Papa Johns currently has ~2.6M likes).
- Set the social media account's setting to require approval if a brand/ person's username is used in a tweet -- this will require the site moderator's approval before it is posted to the official wall or feed.

Relevant Media

Over 11,000 retweets and 260,000 views

Papa John's Facebook Post: "We were extremely concerned to learn of the receipt issue in New York. This act goes against our company values, and we've confirmed with the franchisee that this matter was addressed immediately and that the employee is being terminated. We are truly sorry for this customer's experience."

Most Shared Sources:

Minhee Cho Twitpic
Papa John's Facebook Response
Huffington Post Article

McDonalds Twitter Hashtag Backfires (1)

What Happened:

Relevant Media

- On January 18th, 2012, McDonalds paid Twitter promote the hashtag #McDStories as "trending" on Twitter.
- Around 5 PM, the official McDonalds Twitter account posted the hashtag "McDStories."
- People started using "McDStories" to relate bad experiences about McDonald's and discuss health and safety concerns.
- Within two hours, McDonalds had the hashtag removed due to these negative customer responses.
- On January 18th, the *New York Observer* published the 7 "Best Tweets" of the day around #McDStories.
- On January 24th and 25th, widespread media coverage discussed people's negative use of the #McDStories hashtag.
- Some writers described the campaign as #McFail which itself got over 3,000 posts.

There were **over 20,000 tweets** using the #McDStories hashtag

Most Shared Sources:

NY Times Article

CBS News

Mashable Article

Business Insider Article

McDonalds Twitter Hashtag Backfires (2)

Brand Reaction:

- McDonald's asked Twitter to remove hashtag as trending within two hours.
- They later released a statement that only "2%" of comments were negative and that they had to use their contingency plan to stop promoting hashtag.

Lessons Learned:

- Be aware of customer sentiment before reaching out via social media.
- Hashtags can easily be hijacked.
- Contingency plans for hijacking must always be in place.
- Once the hashtag trends it can be difficult to stop.

Relevant Media

There were **over 20,000 tweets** using the #McDStories hashtag

Most Shared Sources:

NY Times Article

CBS News

Mashable Article

Business Insider Article

Public Outcry Focuses on Pink Slime (1)

What Happened:

- The term "pink slime" was coined in 2002 by Gerald Zirnstein, formerly of the Department of Agriculture. The meat industry refers to it as, "lean finely textured beef."
- Public outcry began in April, 2011 causing thousands of businesses including grocery chains, fast food chains and school districts to discontinue orders of beef containing pink slime.
- Public outcry over pink slime started with celebrity chef Jamie Oliver. On April 12, 2011, a YouTube video of Oliver's television show, *Food Revolution*, was posted and eventually gained over 1.5 million views and 1,500 comments. The season premier featured Oliver demonstrating the process of creating pink slime. Several videos have been posted since and Oliver has also published a blog post summarizing "The Story So Far."

Relevant Media

Most Shared Sources:

Jamie Oliver YouTube Video
Jamie Oliver Blog Post
Bloomberg Article
ABC News Article

Public Outcry Focuses on Pink Slime (2)

Brand Reaction:

- Beef Products Inc. (BPI) and AFA foods suffered significant losses as a result. BPI was forced to shut down 3 of its 4 factories and AFA filed for bankruptcy by April 2012.
- ABC news reported on September 13, 2012, Beef Products Inc. (BPI) was filing a $1.2 billion lawsuit against Zirnstein and ABC news for defamation of their product that was deemed safe for consumption by the USDA.

Lessons Learned:

- The food industry is at high risk for public outrage.
- Remaining transparent and open is key to preventing it.
- When an issue is unavoidable, early warning is critical so that business is prepared to respond to protect its brand as much as possible.

Relevant Media

Most Shared Sources:

Jamie Oliver YouTube Video
Jamie Oliver Blog Post
Bloomberg Article
ABC News Article

ListenLogic
an AKUDA LABS Company

Chick-Fil-A "Hates" Gay Marriage (1)

What Happened:

- LGBT groups lashed out after finding that the company donated approximately $2 million dollars to anti-gay Christian organizations in 2010. Previously Chick-Fil-A had only donated $3 million between 2003 and 2008. This uproar came after years criticism and responses from Dan Cathy, Chick-Fil-A's president.
- A video interview from July 2012 began a much bigger public outrage. The Chick-Fil-A President, made comments about supporting a Christian biblical interpretation of marriage. He offered an apology for the misunderstanding but did not apologize to whom they donated to.
- Chick-Fil-A posted on Facebook about the company staying out of the gay marriage debate and asserting their Christian values. The single post gained over 240,000 "Likes," over 50,000 comments, and 16,000 shares
- Chick-Fil-A supporters started Chick-Fil-A Appreciation Day to counter the movement on August 1, 2012 and had over 650,000 attendees listed on the Facebook event page.

Relevant Media

Most Shared Sources:

Atlanta Journal Constitution Article

LGBTQ Nation Article

Baptist Press Interview

Chick-Fil-A Facebook Post

Chick-Fil-A Tweet

Chick-Fil-A Appreciation Day Facebook Event

Chick-Fil-A Statement

Chick-Fil-A "Hates" Gay Marriage (2)

Brand Reaction:

- After a Chicago politician said in September 2012 that Chick-Fil-A would no longer support anti-gay organizations. Chick-Fil-A released a statement saying that they would focus their giving to, "programs that educate youth, strengthen families and enrich marriages, and support communities." The statement remained unclear on the subject of gay marriage.

Lessons Learned:

- Avoiding polarizing political issues as a corporation is paramount to avoiding social media crisis.
- Many of Chick-Fil-A's PR issues could have been avoided if they had early warning to avoid any statements around the issue.

Relevant Media

Most Shared Sources:

Atlanta Journal Constitution Article

LGBTQ Nation Article

Baptist Press Interview

Chick-Fil-A Facebook Post

Chick-Fil-A Tweet

Chick-Fil-A Appreciation Day Facebook Event

Chick-Fil-A Statement

Not-So-Happy Meal: 4 Years and Counting (1)

What Happened:

- In 1989 Len Foley started the Burger Museum, which boasts the largest 'aged burger' collection in the world. Foley travels with his collection, lecturing about nutrition and health. On February 1, 2007 he posted a video on Youtube which has over 3 million views.
- In 1996, wellness instructor Karen Hanrahan bought a McDonald's Hamburger and has used it as an instructional tool. Hanrahan blogged about it in 2008, as did several other bloggers. It is unclear whether Hanrahan has kept her 1996 burger.
- In 2004, Dr. Oz-endorsed dietician Julia Havey bought a McDonald's hamburger and fries which she uses as teaching tools in her diet lectures. In 2008 Diet.com posted a video interview with Havey. That video received 5 million views.
- On April 10, 2010 Sally Davies began documenting the progress of a McDonald's Happy Meal she intended to monitor for signs of decomposition. Her 'experiment' is now in it's third year.
- These projects have inspired many users to make their own copy-cat videos and post them online.

Relevant Media

Original and copy-cat videos have over **9M Youtube views** since early videos were posted in 2007

7k Facebook Likes

2.8k Tweets

Most Shared Sources:

4 Year Old Hamburger Video

The Happy Meal Project, Flickr

The Burger Museum

Karen Hanrahan Blog

McDonalds Response

Morgan Spurlock Copy-Cat Video

ListenLogic
an AKUDA LABS Compai

Not-So-Happy Meal: 4 Years and Counting (2)

Brand Reaction:

- On October 14, 2010 McDonald's responded to these videos by referring to the cleanliness of their facilities and their high standard of production.
- They also stated that McDonald's products rot and mold 'under the right conditions.'

Lessons Learned:

- Address the specific problem directly, rather than responding with unrelated points.
- Be careful not to bring attention to other incidents with the company in the response.

Relevant Media

Original and copy-cat videos have over **9M Youtube views** since early videos were posted in 2007

7k Facebook Likes

2.8k Tweets

Most Shared Sources:

4 Year Old Hamburger Video

The Happy Meal Project, Flickr

The Burger Museum

Karen Hanrahan Blog

McDonalds Response

Morgan Spurlock Copy-Cat Video

ListenLogic
an AKUDA LABS Company

Oreo Cookie Sparks Gay Rights Debate (1)

What Happened:

- On June 25, 2012 Oreo posted an image of a rainbow version of their cookie on Facebook.
- In one day, there were over 14,000 comments and 140,000 shares
- The posts were both positive and negative as people expressed discontent with their outward support of Gay Pride Day.
- The conversation immediately turned into a debate over religion, family, etc.
- Oreo's post was never removed from their Facebook page.

Brand Reaction:

- An Oreo rep provided a statement:

    "In celebration of the 100th birthday of Oreo cookies, the brand is creating a series of daily ads reflecting current events in a fun way using images of Oreo cookies and milk. .... The new campaign will bring to life trending topics, pop culture news, milestones or celebrations using images of the iconic cookie and milk. In recognition of Pride Month, Oreo created an ad depicting the Rainbow flag with different colors of Oreo crème. We are excited to illustrate what is making history today in a fun and playful way. You can follow Oreo on Facebook to see the daily ads."

Relevant Media

Original Facebook Post has **~300,000 "Likes"**, **60,000 comments**, and **90,000 shares**

Most Shared Sources:

Oreo's Facebook Post

BuzzFeed Article (Includes Sample Facebook Comments)

Mashable Article

72

Oreo Cookie Sparks Gay Rights Debate (2)

Lessons Learned:

- Immediately control the conversation on the corporate social media page.
- Require a second level of verification so that multiple company reps approve the post before it appears -- this will help avoid provocative, negative and offensive content from appearing.
- Do not remove a post after intense objection has been shown as this will appear as backing down after the fact.

Relevant Media

Original Facebook Post has **~300,000 "Likes"**, **60,000 comments**, and **90,000 shares**

Most Shared Sources:

Oreo's Facebook Post

BuzzFeed Article (Includes Sample Facebook Comments)

Mashable Article

ListenLogic
an AKUDA LABS Company

Lude Hack of Mt. Dew Naming Contest

What Happened:

- On August 12th, 2012, Pepsi started an online contest to name their new flavor of Mountain Dew.
- Shortly afterwards, users from sites *4chan* and *Reddit* started discussions encouraging other users to vote for offensive names.
- The site, DubTheDew.com, gave a company-sponsored name "Tempest", but this was quickly outvoted.
- The site was taken down once the voting became out of control.
- On August 14th, Mountain Dew responded via Twitter stating they had "lost to The Internet."

Brand Reaction:

- Mt. Dew attempted to control contest, when this failed, they took down the site and admitted failure.

Lessons Learned:

- People out simply to "troll" on message boards, polls, comments can wreak havoc on a company's innocent intentions.
- Contingency plans must be planned before launching a promotion.

Relevant Media

Over 5,000 comments on various Reddit, 4Chan threads, and **thousands of posts** after media coverage

Most Shared Sources:

TIME Article
Mashable Article
Reddit Thread
Image of Voting
Mountain Dew's
Twitter Post

Maker's Mark's Racist Mess (1)

What Happened:

- On August 17, 2012 Andre Mulligan went to the Maker's Mark Bourbon House and Lounge to discuss a public event taking place the next day.
- Mulligan states that restaurant managers asked about the "the ratio of 'black people' to 'white people' attending the event."
- During the event, Mulligan alleges black people were denied entrance to the venue.
- On August 29, 2012 Mulligan filed suit against Louisville Bourbon and Cordish Operating Ventures (restaurant operator).
- On December 20, 2012 *AlterNet* published an article, bringing broader attention to the issue.
- On December 22, 2012 hacking group Anonymous tweeted about the issue several times.

Relevant Media

Most Shared Sources:

AlertNet Article
Salon.com Article
SignOn Petition
Ace Weekly Article
The Whiskey Reviewer Article
Eater - Louisville Article
Baltimore Sun (Legal Documents)
Maker's Mark Apology
Anonymous Tweet #1
Anonymous Tweet #2

Maker's Mark's Racist Mess (2)

Brand Reaction:

- On December 24, 2012 Maker's Mark issued a statement holding Cordish Operating Ventures accountable for their actions while threatening to act on behalf of their own brand, if necessary.

Lessons Learned:

- Make sure the groups licensing your brand behave according to your brands standards.
- A swift response in sensitive situations is imperative; while Maker's Mark responded quickly after the issue was brought to the public's attention their response still came more than three months after the initial event.

Relevant Media

Most Shared Sources:

AlertNet Article
Salon.com Article
SignOn Petition
Ace Weekly Article
The Whiskey Reviewer Article
Eater - Louisville Article
Baltimore Sun (Legal Documents)
Maker's Mark Apology
Anonymous Tweet #1
Anonymous Tweet #2

Have It Your Way: Burger King's Special Boot Flavoring (1)

What Happened:

- The user posted the photo on *4chan* on July 16 at 11:38 p.m.
- That same night at 11:47 p.m., another *4chan* user noted that the photo's Exif data pointed to Mayfield Heights, Ohio.
- 12 minutes later, someone posted the address of the Burger King branch in which the lettuce-stepping occurred, wishing the original poster a 'happy unemployment.'
- At 11:55 p.m. someone contacted the news and posted on their Facebook page.
- At 11:58 p.m., someone posted the link to Burger King's Tell Us About Us form, with the photo attached.
- Around midnight, a *4chan* user contacted the manager at Burger King about the situation, ultimately sending the photo.
- Morning of July 17, *Cleveland Scene Magazine* and *The Huffington Post* contacted the Burger King franchise, talking to the morning manager:

  "Whoever this is is getting fired...And whoever the manager was at the time will be fired, too."

Relevant Media

Most Shared Sources:

Incident Photo

4Chan Message Board Screenshot

Mashable Article

Have It Your Way: Burger King's
Special Boot Flavoring (2)

Brand Reaction:

- The night manager responded to the *4chan* user saying that he will find out the person and disciplinary action will be taken.
- After the breakfast shift manager was contacted the next morning by the press about the photo, the employee was identified and terminated.
- *Fox 8 News* received a statement from Burger King's Manager of Global Communications, Denise Wilson stating that food safety is most important and doesn't condone these actions. She said this is a franchise and the owner is taking care of the situation.

Lessons Learned:

- Video and images posted on the web will be produced and exist in the digital space forever if they are immediately intercepted.
- Blogs and forums often have strong followings of users that are very active and will spread the incident across multiple mediums very quickly.

Relevant Media

Most Shared Sources:

Incident Photo

4Chan Message Board Screenshot

Mashable Article

Taco Bell Worker Designs New Menu Item: Urine Nachos (1)

What Happened:

- Early morning August 2, 2012 a Fort Wayne, IN Taco Bell employee, Cameron Jankowski, tweeted picture of himself urinating on nachos to @huntermoore, a porn website magnate (115,000 followers):

  "@Huntermoore @is_anyone_up guess where I work. #pissolympics #nachobellgrande http://t.co/VLmyQJtQ"

- A few hours later around 4:30 AM, Moore awarded him "winner of the piss Olympics", asking his followers:

  "What else should @Cameronisonfire piss in at work"

- Around 1:30 PM that day, hacking group Anonymous leaked his personal information and asked their significant following to spread the video they had created with the info (it has since been removed):

  "Find This Taco Bell Employee Peeing In Food - SPREAD THIS VIDEO | http://bit.ly/OLKySW"

- Later in the day, *Indiana's NewsCenter* alerted Taco Bell and the health department of the tweet.

Relevant Media

Most Shared Sources:

Indiana's NewsCenter Article

Huffington Post Article

Gawker Article

Taco Bell Worker Designs New Menu Item: Urine Nachos (2)

Brand Reaction:

- Taco Bell responded to *Indiana's NewsCenter* call about the issue stating food safety is most important to the restaurant. They also noted that it was in fact a prank but that the employee would be fired and they plan to pursue legal action.
- They also plan to shut down the location for food safety training for employees.

Lessons Learned:

- Video and images posted on the web will be reproduced and exist in the digital space forever -- they also provide concrete proof of an action.
- Tweeting at an influential figure without knowing their reach or who is watching their Twitter feed is dangerous -- in this case, it brought the largest hacking group in the world into the matter, which ultimately got the police involved.

Relevant Media

Most Shared Sources:

Indiana's NewsCenter Article

Huffington Post Article

Gawker Article

ListenLogic
an AKUDA LABS Compa

McDonald's Employees Share Horror Stories Online (1)

What Happened:

- In June 2012, a McDonald's employee shared his experiences working there on the popular Internet site, *Reddit*, as an AMA (Ask Me Anything) where *Reddit* users can ask questions and the employee responds.
- The thread received over 2,500 comments, and 2,000 "up votes."
- The user posted about customers throwing ice cream at him, cursing at him, and people paying with McDonald's game money. He also discussed how they deal with customers that are drunk or on drugs.
- Overall this employee shared both positive and negative stories and said he likes his job.
- Starting on June 27, the thread began to receive national media attention when *The Atlantic* wrote an article about it.
- *The Huffington Post* wrote about it on June 28th, and the *LA Times* on June 29th.
- Another *Reddit* thread was started around the same time from a McDonald's employee sharing the worst customer service stories they had experienced.
- This subsequent thread received over 6,500 comments and 4,500 "up votes."

Relevant Media

The 2 Reddit threads combined received **over 9,000 comments & 6,500 "up votes"**

Most Shared Sources:

Reddit Thread (Original)

The Atlantic Article

Huffington Post Article

LA Times Article

ListenLogic
an AKUDA LABS Company

McDonald's Employees Share Horror Stories Online (2)

Brand Reaction:

- A McDonald's spokeswoman responded to the *LA Times* saying:

    "While this crew member is not a spokesperson for McDonald's, as with any job, I think we can all agree there are ups and downs, good days and bad. We believe these posts reflect that."

Lessons Learned:

- Any company who has workers that deal with a lot of customers should expect that at some point they will have an employee that goes online to discuss their experiences.
- Because of the anonymity of the Internet, employees will feel like they can share how they feel without any consequences so companies must have a plan in place and be prepared to respond to things like this.

Relevant Media

The 2 Reddit threads combined received **over 9,000 comments & 6,500 "up votes"**

Most Shared Sources:

Reddit Thread (Original)

The Atlantic Article

Huffington Post Article

LA Times Article

Greenpeace Takes on Palm Oil in KitKat (1)

What Happened:

- On March 17, 2010, Greenpeace released a blog post and an ad on YouTube targeting Nestlé for palm oil production harming rainforests in Asia. The ad was viewed an estimated 1.5 million times.
- Nestlé reportedly had the ad removed for copyright infringement but was reposted on Vimeo and continued being reposted on YouTube.
- After Nestlé promised to protect the rainforests, Greenpeace published a blog post about their success which gained nearly 9,000 Facebook "Likes".

Relevant Media

Most Shared Sources:

YouTube Video

Greenpeace Initial Blog Post

Vimeo Video

Nestlé Response on Facebook

Greenpeace Success Blog Post

Greenpeace Takes on Palm Oil in KitKat (2)

Brand Reaction:

- Nestle removed the ad from YouTube but later retracted their copyright infringement claim.
- Nestlé used their Facebook page to discuss the issue with consumers. Eight wall posts were written by Nestlé between March 17th and May 16th with which hundreds of people posted inflammatory comments that criticized the company after Facebook page manager responded inappropriately to several of them.
- Nestle Facebook page manager apologized for his/her remarks.
- Nestle later announced a "zero-deforestation" policy in conjunction with The Forest Trust.

Lessons Learned:

- Consumer groups have significant power over consumers' perception of an issue and can leverage those consumers to attack your company.

Relevant Media

Most Shared Sources:

YouTube Video

Greenpeace Initial Blog Post

Vimeo Video

Nestlé Response on Facebook

Greenpeace Success Blog Post

Doritos Pulls Catholic Commercial From Superbowl Contest

What Happened:

- In November 2010, Media Wave Productions submitted a commercial for the "Doritos Crash the SuperBowl" contest.
- The ad featured a pastor who used Doritos and Pepsi MAX for communion in order to attract more churchgoers.
- After it was published on Pepsi's website, it was quickly removed after many Catholic groups contacted PepsiCo. directly as a result of petitions on Americaneedsfatima.org and other sites.
- President of Media Wave Productions, Dave Williams, later said, "We felt bad...Our intention was to win, not to offend."
- The spot was published on YouTube by MWP on December 26, 2010 and has been viewed over 200,000 times and commented on nearly 3,000 times. Despite the Catholic backlash, "likes" outweighed "dislikes" by a ratio of 4 to 1.

Relevant Media

Most Shared Sources:

Petition

Mashable Article

USA Today Article

YouTube Video

Doritos Pulls Catholic Commercial From Superbowl Contest

Brand Reaction:

- Commercial was not included in the final 10 videos for the contest.
- Pepsi apologized to anyone who was offended.

Lessons Learned:

- Have methods of screening video content in contests.
- Explicitly tell people the rules and the contest but remember that 1st amendment rights may always arise.

Relevant Media

Most Shared Sources:

Petition
Mashable Article
USA Today Article
YouTube Video

ListenLogic
an AKUDA LABS Compan

Greenpeace Targets KFC Box Materials

What Happened:

- In late May, 2012 Greenpeace published a reported claiming that KFC and its parent company, Yum! Brands is using rain-forest wood in their boxes.
- The report then claimed that this has major effects on the region and species inhabiting Indonesia.
- They named Asia Pulp & Paper and Yum! Brands as those responsible.
- This sparked massive environmental discussion on the Web and Greenpeace activists hung a sign on Yum!'s headquarters in Louisville, KY in protest.
- APP vowed to halt all natural forest clearance by June 1, 2012.
- Greenpeace responded stating that this date keeps being pushed back.

Brand Reaction:

- Yum! Brands commented that its suppliers aim for 60% purchasing from sustainable forests, but aim for 100%.
- APP stated on May 23, 2012 that it "deplores this distortion of the facts by Greenpeace."
- APP also defended their practices, stating they follow all current legal and industry requirements.

Lessons Learned:

- Environmental activists have a strong following, are active online and often take action to prove a point -- try to deal with them directly before the issue spreads and the story is distorted on social media.

Relevant Media

Most Shared Sources:

Daily Mail (UK) Article

Bloomberg Article

Greenpeace Blog

Subway's Facebook Trolled With Adult-Themed Cartoons (NSFW)

What Happened:

- Fans of "an animated pop star in Japan," Miku Hatsune, began incorporating Subway sandwiches into Hentai (porn comics) in December 2011. The idea originated from a FacePunch.com photoshop contest called, "Photoshop Subways Sandwiches Into Hentai comics," and Miku Hatsune fan pages on Twitter, Facebook, Tumblr, and Google+.
- The administrator of the Miku Hatsune fan pages then suggested that the pictures should be posted on Subway's Facebook.
- On August 15, 2012, fans began posting dozens of the photos on Subway's Facebook photo section. By the afternoon, Subway's Facebook moderator noticed the posts and began removing them, but posters continued to post them.

Brand Reaction:

- Subway deleted all associated content by that day and banned all participants from accessing their page.
- Subway spokesperson stated they removed the all the posts and are working with Facebook to investigate and resolve the issue.

Lessons Learned:

- Have a means of monitoring and early detection. Understand who's targeting your brand and be ready to mitigate the damage that 'trolling' can cause.

Relevant Media

Most Shared Sources:

Facebook (Hatsune Miku Troll)

FacePunch Thread

Reddit Threads (Sharing Articles)

Mashable Article

The Daily Dot Article

88

Applebee's Waitress Fired Over Reddit Post

What Happened:

- St. Louis Applebee's waitress Chelsea Welch received a signed bill from a customer (part of a party of 20 who split the check) who refused to pay the customary 18% tip added to large parties.
- This customer, pastor Alois Bell, left 0 tip, writing instead: "I give God 10% why do you get 18."
- The waitress posted a photo of the check to *Reddit*.
- The waitress was subsequently fired after her post became popular, when the pastor saw it online and called the Applebee's location.
- There was a massive public response to her firing, and international media covered her story.

Brand Reaction:

- Applebee's fired the employee for posting the photo on *Reddit* (employee claims she did nothing illegal, "there was nothing specific in the employee handbook admonishing this behavior," and took every measure to keep the pastor's identity anonymous).

Lessons Learned:

- The Internet community reacted sympathetically to the waitress over the original post.
- Applebee's ignored the public sentiment and their firing of the waitress caused the story to become more popular than the original photo itself.
- Internet communities are a realistic gauge of public appeal.

Relevant Media

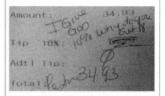

Most Shared Sources:

Gawker Article

Yahoo! Article

Huffington Post

Buzzfeed Article

The Guardian (waitress)

Reddit (fired)

Reddit (original)

Kidney Fried Chicken

What Happened:

- On January 6, 2013, UK student Ibrahim Langoo found a foreign body in a piece of chicken at a KFC in Colchester.
- Langoo posted pictures of it on facebook, and filed a complaint on the KFC website.
- The pictures were shared on the internet and Langoo's story was covered by multiple international news sources.

Brand Reaction:

- KFC experts examined the photo of what was thought to be a brain, but declared that it was most likely a chicken kidney that had not been removed in the preparation process.
- A KFC spokesperson issued the following statement: "We always try to ensure the highest standards in all of our restaurants... We're very sorry about Mr Langoo's experience and while there was no health risk, we agree it was unsightly. We will be carrying out a full investigation and providing him with a gesture of goodwill."
- A KFC representative told *The Sun* (UK) that the photo "likely [undid] millions of dollars in KFC advertising."
- KFC provided Langoo with an undisclosed amount of KFC vouchers.

Lessons Learned:

- Sharing of quality control failures on social media poses an immense threat to brands' reputation and finances.

Relevant Media

Most Shared Sources:

The Sun (UK)

The Daily Mail (UK)

Huffington Post Article

Mashable Article

MSN Article

Redditor Gets Screwed at Moes

What Happened:

- On December 2, 2012, Redditor "vyqz" started a thread in the "/WTF" subforum of *Reddit* linking to a picture of a screw he found in his burrito at Moe's Southwest Grill.
- Another Redditor, "GammaUnit01" later responded by also posting a picture of himself holding a screw he found in his food from Moe's.
- The thread received over 700 comments, ~11,000 up-votes and ~9,000 down votes.

Brand Reaction:

- Moe's did not make a formal response to the *Reddit* thread nor in the media.
- Redditor "vyqz" posted that he "got some free queso" from the staff at the restaurant in which he ate.

Lessons Learned:

- Although neither picture of the screws received national media attention requiring an official response from the Moe's company, the incident proves that a post of this nature to a *Reddit* thread can still be seen by tens of thousands of people in a very short time.

Relevant Media

Most Shared Sources:

Reddit Thread

Angry Mothers Disrupt Dr. Pepper Campaign

What Happened:

- On July 14, 2010, a Coca-Cola promotional campaign required participants to allow the company to post status updates to their Facebook page containing embarrassing and funny messages.
- One referenced a pornographic video in a status update for a 14 year old girl participating in the Dr. Pepper promotion. This caused the girl to search for the video online, but was inhibited by parental controls. She was reportedly one of over 160,000 participants.
- Two days later the girls mother posted an angry message on Mumsnet, a parent networking site, which gained over 1,400 replies discussing the issue.

Brand Reaction:

- Coca-Cola first offered a hotel stay and theatre tickets in London but the mother declined saying it was useless to her because she lived in Glasgow.
- Coca-Cola apologized for the post saying they had approved it without knowing the meaning behind it. It was immediately removed and they decided to end the promotion.
- Their statement said that they were investigating their promotional practices and assured consumers that this would not happen again.

Lessons Learned:

- Unconventional promotions carry a great deal of risk, especially when paired with an outside contractor. Make sure to have safeguards in place to minimize risk.

Relevant Media

Most Shared Sources:

Mumsnet Message Board Post

CBS Article

The Guardian Article

The Telegraph Article

Cracked Blog Post

Starbucks Customer Receives Coffee With A Nasty Note (1)

What Happened:

- In September 2011, a customer made light of a mistake made by a Starbucks barista. The customer, Vicki Reveron, then brought her coffee back to her office and discovered what looked like the word "bitch" written on her cup.
- She went back to the store and showed the manager who responded by saying it was a mistake.
- The manager agreed to give her back the cup along with vouchers for free coffee as long as she did not associate the cup with the Starbucks location.
- As Reveron left, an employee reportedly said out loud, "Some people will do anything to get a free cup of coffee."
- ABC questioned the manager, then sent a picture of the cup to Starbucks Corporate Communications in Seattle. They did not admit that they believed the writing was profane but did say, "We have apologized numerous times for this unfortunate misunderstanding."
- *The Huffington Post* article was shared over 10,000 times on Facebook.

Relevant Media

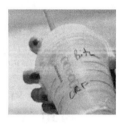

Most Shared Sources:

Original ABC Article

Huffington Post Article

Starbucks Customer Receives Coffee With A Nasty Note (2)

Brand Reaction:

- When the customer complained to the store, they gave her free coffee vouchers which she reportedly doesn't plan on redeeming.
- When leaving the store an employee said, "Some people will do anything to get a free cup of coffee."
- Starbucks spokesperson said, "We have apologized numerous times for this unfortunate misunderstanding."

Lessons Learned:

- Immediately provide a statement and apology when customer service issues arise. The unhappy customer(s) can do much more damage with social media on their side.
- Reinforce corporate policy across all social media platforms.

Relevant Media

Most Shared Sources:

Original ABC Article
Huffington Post Article

Viral Embarrassment: "United Breaks Guitars" (1)

What Happened:

- Baggage handlers destroyed passenger Dave Carroll's guitar on March 31, 2008 in Omaha, NE.
- That same day he told three different United employees who brushed him off, one said, "But hun, that's why we make you sign the waiver"
- After 9 months of back and forth phone calls and emails with United, Carroll was ultimately denied and given five reasons, three of which told him he didn't do things that he claims he did.
- He told United's Ms. Irlweg (who denied the refund and ended communication) that he would produce three songs about his experience to offer for free download on YouTube, goal of 1 million views in one year.
- He created three songs and music videos that are on YouTube, and offered a detailed story of the incident in a blog post.
- Carroll teamed up with a few others and started "GrapeVine," which helps web users connect directly to companies to resolve issues/disputes.

Relevant Media

All 3 YouTube videos **viewed ~14.5M times**
Over **1M tweets** referencing Dave Carroll

Most Shared Sources:

NY Times Article
Dave Carroll's Blog Post
YouTube Video
YouTube Video 2
YouTube Video 3

Viral Embarrassment: "United Breaks Guitars" (2)

Brand Reaction:

- United initially denied his claim multiple times over a nine month period.
- After the videos went viral on YouTube, United apologized and offered flight vouchers and compensation for the repair costs.
- Carroll denied the offer, telling them to give the money to charity.

Lessons Learned:

- If United had resolved the issue within the first few months, Carroll could have been managed before he agreed to make the videos.
- If a customer is denied, do not deny him again when he tells you he is going to create a series of videos attacking the company on YouTube (double deviation).
- Unique music and videos that are supplemented by blog posts and social media become uncontrollable once they're posted online.

Relevant Media

All 3 YouTube videos **viewed ~14.5M times**

Over **1M tweets** referencing Dave Carroll

Most Shared Sources:

NY Times Article

Dave Carroll's Blog Post

YouTube Video

YouTube Video 2

YouTube Video 3

Southwest Promotion: Sign-Up, Pay Us Double (1)

What Happened:

- On August 3rd, 2012, Southwest announced a Facebook promotion to celebrate 3 million Facebook "likes" on their page .
- The promotion garnered a lot of attention and so many people took advantage of it that it caused performance issues on Southwest's website.
- Some customers were subsequently charged more than once for the same reservation,
- Many people publicly complained on Southwest's Facebook page and shared how much they were charged.

Brand Reaction:

- Later in the day, on August 3rd, Southwest updated their Twitter and Facebook accounts saying they were aware of the issues and were working to reverse the charges.
- On August 4th, they provided an explanation on Facebook of what they were doing to correct the issue, including refunding all people charged more than once and paying for any overdraft fees anyone incurred because of their error.

Relevant Media

Over **2,500 comments** and **10,000 "Likes"** on Southwest's Facebook posts about the incident

Most Shared Sources:

Southwest's FB Post
CNN Blog Post
Forbes Article

Southwest Promotion: Sign-Up, Pay Us Double (2)

Lessons Learned:

- When running a promotion over social media it is vital that a company is prepared to handle the response to the promotion, otherwise the promotion ends up quickly bringing negative attention to the company.
- Always have a plan to respond on social media when something does go wrong. In this case, Southwest waited until the end of the day on August 3rd to respond, instead of letting customers know right away.

Relevant Media

Southwest Airlines
August 3 via

Thank you for your excitement in taking advantage of the limited-time offer we shared today in celebration of reaching three million Fans on Facebook. Due to the overwhelming response, we experienced some site performance issues at various times throughout the day. We apologize to our Customers for any inconvenience and are proactively cancelling any duplicate itineraries that may have occurred.

Like Comment Share

Over **2,500 comments** and **10,000 "Likes"** on Southwest's Facebook posts about the incident

Most Shared Sources:

Southwest's FB Post
CNN Blog Post
Forbes Article

JetBlue Flight Attendant Freakout

What Happened:

- On August 9, 2010, JetBlue Flight Attendant Steven Slater got into an argument with a passenger right after the plane landed, used profanity towards the passengers and said he quit, grabbed two beers, and deployed the planes escape chute and slid down and exited the plane.
- Over the next few days the story received mainstream media attention from *USA Today*, *Wall Street Journal*, and *New York Times,* among many others.
- The attention led to Slater becoming a "cult hero" on social media with various Facebook fan pages, becoming a trending topic on Twitter, and with numerous YouTube videos/songs written about him.

Brand Reaction:

- JetBlue first commented on the incident on its blog mentioning how "the entire Internet" was talking about it.
- JetBlue sent a memo to its employees discouraging them from similar actions.
- CEO David Barger criticized Steven Slater for acting poorly and disagreed with his portrayal as a hero.

Lessons Learned:

- Slater's actions were unpredictable but the response on social media was even more surprising. If JetBlue had been monitoring their social media risks, they could have identified the event before it became national news.

Relevant Media

The most popular song supporting Slater on YouTube has over **100,000 views**

The most popular Steven Slater Facebook fan page has over **178,000 "Likes"**

Most Shared Sources:

Facebook Fan Page

YouTube Video

Huffington Post Article

JetBlue Blog Response

Alec Baldwin Just Wants Some 'Words With Friends' (1)

What Happened:

- December 6, 2011 Alec Baldwin was kicked off an American Airlines flight while the plane was idling at the gate.
- Alec Baldwin tweeted that it was because he was playing the game 'Words with Friends':

   "Flight attendant on American reamed me out 4 playing WORDS W FRIENDS while we sat at the gate, not moving. #nowonderamericaairisbankrupt"

   "Now, as I was kicked off this flight, the word I was playing was UNITED"

- AA reached out to Baldwin on Twitter the same day to have him contact with a direct message.
- The next day, Baldwin wrote a piece in *The Huffington Post* travel section discussing his grievances and issues on the AA flight the day before.

Relevant Media

Most Shared Sources:

Inquirer Article

CNET Article

Engadget Article

Letsrollforums.com Forum Post

ListenLogic
an AKUDA LABS Company

Alec Baldwin Just Wants Some 'Words With Friends' (2)

Brand Reaction:

- American Airlines tweeted to Alec Baldwin:

    "Comment on something that might or might not have happened"

- They then posted on Facebook describing their version of the story to the public, regarding FAA regulations, etc.

Lessons Learned:

- When an influential person posts on one social media platform, do not use another site to air grievances or explanations -- it will bring an entirely different following of people into the discussion.
- Be clear with the reasoning for dismissing the client and try to quietly resolve the issue (in this case on Twitter), before entire followings of people and mainstream media start forming perceptions.

Relevant Media

Most Shared Sources:

Inquirer Article

CNET Article

Engadget Article

Letsrollforums.com Forum Post

Southwest Airlines' Too Fat to Fly (1)

What Happened:

- On February 13, 2010, Southwest removed Kevin Smith (Writer/Director/Producer) from their flight saying he needed to purchase a second seat in order to remain on the plane due to a "Customer Size" Policy.
- Kevin Smith tweeted at Southwest about the issue, sharing it with all his over 2.1 million followers. Smith continued to tweet until after he arrived at his destination. Southwest responded on Twitter eight times. Smith's tweets were retweeted nearly 500 times and "favorited" over 200 times.
- A twitpic posted on February 15 of him on the plane with the caption, "Hey @SouthwestAir! Look how fat I am on your plane! Quick! Throw me off!" was viewed over 150,000 times and gained over 175 comments.

Relevant Media

Most Shared Sources:

Kevin Smith Original Tweet

Kevin Smith Twitpic

Southwest Blog Post

Kevin Smith Response Blog Post

Southwest Airlines' Too Fat to Fly (2)

Brand Reaction:

- In less than 20 minutes after Smith's initial tweet, Southwest started responding on Twitter. An attempt was made to contact Kevin Smith on the phone the night of the incident.
- On February 15, 2010, Southwest released a public blog post written by the Vice President of Corporate Communications & Strategic Outreach. The post apologized to Smith and mentioned their February 15th phone call in which they notified him that his airfare was complimentary. Over 1,800 comments were left on the blog post, over 2,000 "LUV its," and over 300 shared the blog post on Twitter.

Lessons Learned:

- Policies can quickly become the focus of public scrutiny when it is criticized on social media.
- Influential people can quickly affect PR, and ultimately business. While celebrities may have more direct influence on a company with customer service issues, everyone else can indirectly affect a company in the same way if the right people see it.

Relevant Media

Most Shared Sources:

Kevin Smith Original Tweet

Kevin Smith Twitpic

Southwest Blog Post

Kevin Smith Response Blog Post

Southwest Kicks Green Day Band Member Off Flight

What Happened:

- On September 1, 2011, Southwest kicked Green Day band member Billie Joe Armstrong off flight because of saggy pants. The person he was travelling with was also removed.
- Armstrong's angry tweet about the incident was retweeted nearly 5,000 times and over 2,500 people marked it as a "favorite."
- Armstrong took the next flight to Burbank, CA from Oakland, CA.

Brand Reaction:

- In a little over an hour, Southwest tweeted: "@BJAofficial Very sorry for your experience tonight, someone from our Customer Relations Team will reach out to you to get more details."

Lessons Learned:

- The service industry is at the mercy of celebrities and online influencers. Much damage can be done in a small amount of time if the wrong people hear about an issue such as this.
- Understand the potential reach and damage that influential users have on Twitter, Facebook, and other high-traffic sites.

Relevant Media

Most Shared Sources:

Billie Joe Armstrong Original Tweet

Southwest Airlines Tweet

Huffington Post Article

ListenLogic
an AKUDA LABS Company

104

United Airlines Loses Unaccompanied Minor (1)

What Happened:

- In June, 2012, United Airlines lost 10-year old Phoebe Klehban in Chicago.
- United reportedly denied Phoebe's request to call her parents three times after a third party unaccompanied minor escort "forgot" to show up. Then after United was contacted, they insisted the daughter must be in Michigan.
- After over an hour, The Klehbans finally got a United employee to find Phoebe and talked to her on the phone.
- Four hours later, they got her to Michigan, but her bags were lost and took three days to get them to her.
- United denied their request to file a complaint letter and instead wrote what the Kelhbans told the employee over the phone.
- They then sent a letter to the CEO and after being denied all requests, they contacted a local NBC station who then reached out to United.
- A friend of the Klehban's, Robert Sutton (a Stanford professor, author and contributor to *The Huffington Post*) posted on his blog, with a direct link to the letter that they wrote to the CEO.

Relevant Media

Most Shared Sources:

Bob Sutton Blog

Huffington Post Article

Gawker Article

Today Show Video

United Airlines Loses Unaccompanied Minor (2)

Brand Reaction:

- Only after the NBC reporter contacted United, did an executive contact them to resolve the issue.
- United apologized to the family and commented in the news after the whole ordeal was completed.
- They refunded the Kelhban's miles and the unaccompanied minor fee.

Lessons Learned:

- Directly work with consumers before they go to the news, double deviation in customer service (especially with airline travel) can cause tremendous hardship to companies.
- There are particular sensitivities when children are involved in an incident.
- Deception often creates significantly more issues for the corporation than a straight-forward response.

Relevant Media

Most Shared Sources:

Bob Sutton Blog
Huffington Post Article
Gawker Article
Today Show Video

American Airlines Responds to Every Tweet

What Happened:

- American Airlines had set up polite automated responses for any tweets addressed to @AmericanAir.
- Some people received these cordial responses after having tweeted complains about the airline, prompting others to do the same just to receive the automatic replies that didn't make sense in context.

Brand Reaction:

- American Airlines deleted some negative tweets that received polite auto-responses.
- American Airlines tweeted at some of the users who had complained and received polite replies: "Please let us know if we can help in any way."

Lessons Learned:

- Automatic reply tweets can result in creating further dissatisfaction with upset customers. They can also lead damage to the brand. A company should take into account the kinds of tweets they will receive before setting up automatic responses.

Relevant Media

Most Shared Sources:

Business Insider

British Airways Approves Racist Tweet

What Happened:

- On November 17, 2012 an irate customer posted to @British_Airways, their displeasure that the airline had cancelled their flight.
- A user, "Asian Ronaldo" then responded to the original user with an offensive, racial slur and was retweeted by British Airways' Twitter account.
- That post was then posted to the official Twitter feed of British Airways.
- Immediate backlash occurred that night as #BritishAirways was trending on Twitter in less than 24 hours.
- Users on the site couldn't figure out if the post was a hoax or legitimate until British Airways responded.

Brand Reaction:

- British Airways commented on November 18, 2012, apologizing for the incident:

  > *"Apologies for the last RT. We are sorry for any offence caused and are investigating how this may have happened."*

- British Airways then continuously responded to users commenting on their apologetic post.

Lessons Learned:

- Always have content approved and monitored by an accountable person to ensure that nothing offensive appears on official corporate accounts.
- Track and monitor issues after the fact, to perform damage control and keep a company from ultimately trending on a social media platform.

Relevant Media

Asian Ronaldo @GordonQiu9   51m
"@JaeLadd: @British_Airways ▓▓▓ you. ▓▓▓▓ cancelling my flight! #bunchof▓▓▓▓"go back to your ▓▓▓ country you ▓▓▓

Most Shared Sources:

Daily Mail (UK) Article

The Independent (UK) Article

Needles Found in Sandwiches on Delta Flight (1)

What Happened:

- On July 15, 2012, a passenger on a Delta flight from Amsterdam bit down on a needle hidden in their sandwich. Sewing needles were found in a total of 5 sandwiches.
- Delta announced within hours that they and the FBI were investigating all the incidents and Delta contacted all flights coming from Amsterdam to not serve the sandwiches.
- Delta began serving prepackaged food instead and did not find any more needles.
- On July 17, 2012, the customer that bit down on the sandwich and another that found a needle on the same flight were interviewed by *ABC News*. The second customer said that he called his wife who was on another outbound flight from Amsterdam and learned that his son had also found a needle in his sandwich.
- The next day, the customer injured by a needle was also featured in a *Guardian* video discussing the incident, the investigation, and the food company that prepared the food, Gate Gourmet.

Relevant Media

Most Shared Sources:

ABC News Video

The Guardian Video

Huffington Post Article

Needles Found in Sandwiches on Delta Flight (2)

Brand Reaction:

- The airline made a statement and replaced the sandwiches with prepackaged food and began an investigation into the source of the needles.

Lessons Learned:

- A swift and decisive reaction is good, especially during ongoing controversy. A quick response is paramount to diminishing public criticism.

Relevant Media

Needle found by MSP Customs B.

Most Shared Sources:

ABC News Video

The Guardian Video

Huffington Post Article

Carnival Cruise Fails At Trying To Shut Down Social Media

What Happened:

- On January 13th, 2012, a Costa Cruise ship ran aground, resulting in the death of 32 passengers.
- In the following week, Costa Cruise's parent company, Carnival Cruise received much of the blame and criticism.
- On January 19th, 2012, Carnival Cruise announced via Facebook it was "going to take a bit of a break from posting on our social channels."
- Customers responded very negatively, and this caused further criticism of Carnival.
- On January 24th, 2012, said it would "resume" social media communication.
- This announcement was also criticized by customers, and various articles.

Brand Reaction:

- Carnival shut down social media interaction during the height of the crisis.
- Carnival then opened up communication via social media a week later.

Lessons Learned:

- Customers expect increased engagement in times of crisis.
- Social media discussion of companies will occur regardless if the company participates.
- Failing to participate in these discussions can be one of the worst options.

Relevant Media

Over 8,000 "Likes" and **1,400 comments** on Carnival's Facebook posts

Most Shared Sources:

Carnival "Shutting Down" Facebook Post

Carnival "Re-Engaging" Announcement Facebook Post

Ad Age Article

Special Delivery: FedEx Pitches Package Over Gate

What Happened:

- On December 19, 2011 a YouTube video was posted showing security footage of FedEx throwing a boxed computer monitor over a fence. That same day the video was shared via *Reddit* and Facebook.
- On December 20 and 21 the video was shared via *The Huffington Post*, Yahoo!, and ComedyCentral, among others.
- The video was categorized as "News & Politics."

Brand Reaction:

- On December 21, 2011 FedEx posted a video featuring their SVP of Operations apologizing.
- They have reached out to the customer and replaced the monitor.

Lessons Learned:

- Focus on showing the viewers and social media world that this video doesn't represent the company as a whole.
- Create positive YouTube videos of customers pleased with the service.
- Respond quickly and in-kind.

Relevant Media

Over 8.8 Million views for original video on YouTube

Over 500,000 views on FedEx's response video

Most Shared Sources:

YouTube Video (Security Footage)
YouTube Video (FedEx Response)
Reddit Threads
Mashable Article
Daily Mail Article

CEO Pays Insured $118k After Exchange on Twitter (1)

What Happened:

Relevant Media

- In February 2012, Arijit Guha created the Twitter account, @poop_strong, and poopstrong.org to raise money for his medical bills.
- In April, Arijit Guha tweeted about Aetna refusing to pay his remaining medical bills of $118,000 after paying the maximum $300,000 lifetime cap.
- On July 22nd, Guha and others directly criticized Aetna and the CEO on Twitter for their low caps.
- On July 26th, Aetna CEO, Mark T. Bertolini, chose to respond to several criticisms, including Guha's, on Twitter which inflamed supporters even more.
- Guha's friend Jen Wang posted the Twitter communications between Aetna, Bertolini, Guha, and his supporters on Storify which was viewed over 33,000 times.

Most Shared Sources:

Arijit Guha's Original Tweet

Arijit Guha's Tweet to Aetna and its CEO

Poopstrong.org

Arijit Guha's Thank You Tweet

Jen Wang's Storify

NY Times Blog Post

CEO Pays Insured $118k After Exchange on Twitter (2)

Brand Reaction:

- On August 3rd, Bertolini agreed that Aetna would cover Guha's remaining medical bills and the $130,000 raised on poopstrong.org was re-allocated to charity.
- As a result, Aetna will offer a student plan with no lifetime cap and a $2 million annual cap that will eventually disappear under the Affordable Care Act. The policy covers preventive care and doesn't deny students with pre-existing conditions and will be available for the 2012-13 school year at Arizona State University.
- Bertolini later said in an e-mail detailed on the *New York Times* blog that, "This was a compelling case...This felt like a discussion I should be involved in. I appreciated the conversation, even when it was pointed." He further noted he was, "pleased we found a resolution, working with the school, to help him."

Lessons Learned:

- Social media and the rise of Internet use makes executives much more visible and vulnerable to the public. This may hurt a corporation as much as it can benefit them in regards to public relations.
- Expect consumers to leverage social media to make their complaints heard.

Relevant Media

Most Shared Sources:

Arijit Guha's Original Tweet

Arijit Guha's Tweet to Aetna and its CEO

Poopstrong.org

Arijit Guha's Thank You Tweet

Jen Wang's Storify

NY Times Blog Post

Motrin Ad Offends Mothers

What Happened:

- In November, 2008 Motrin released ad targeting mothers who carried their babies.
- Ad was perceived as offensive to mothers.
- Throughout November of 2008, mothers responded by using Twitter hashtag #motrinmoms to criticize the advertisement and the Motrin brand.
- By mid-November McNeil Consumer Healthcare, who makes Motrin, took down the ad down from the Motrin site.
- McNeil's director of communications also apologized for offending people with the advertisement.

Brand Reaction:

- McNeil prepared a statement, removed the ad from its website.
- They also apologized that current print had already been released with the content.

Lessons Learned:

- Make sure no social group is offended by advertising content.
- Be aware of how your intended audience is reacting to your message.

Relevant Media

YouTube videos combined have been **viewed over 500,000 times**

Most Shared Sources:

Motrin Advertisement Example of "Angry Mom"

Scientific American (McNeil Response)

Bitter Pills: J&J Recalls Products

What Happened:

- In January, 2010 J&J began a series of rolling recalls that would plague the company for years to come.
- In 2010 J&J issued 13 separate recalls. Products included Tylenol, Motrin, Rolaids, SimplySleep, Benadryl, Snt. Joseph's.
- In 2011 J&J issued 6 separate recalls. Products included Tylenol, Benadryl, Sudafed, Rolaids, Sinutab, Motrin IB.
- In 2012 J&J issued 2 separate recalls. Products included Tylenol, Immodium.

Brand Reaction:

- In April 2012, former J&J CEO Bill Weldon took responsibility for recalls and stepped down.
- In February 2012, new CEO, Alex Gorsky, vowed to remove known carcinogens from certain products.
- In September 2012, Sandra Peterson was appointed as the new Group Worldwide Chairman, a new position designed to improve manufacturing and supply chain.

Lessons Learned:

- Health recalls must be managed internally, without providing excess worrisome information to consumers.
- Prove that measures are being taken to keep this incident from occurring again.

Relevant Media

Most Shared Sources:

Sac Bee Article

AdWeek Article

ABC News Article

Forbes Article

BP Permanently Plagues Gulf of Mexico (1)

What Happened:

- British Petroleum had numerous lawsuits and safety concerns around their deep sea drilling business -- then on April 10, 2010 the Deepwater Horizon rig exploded, leaking uncontrollable amounts of oil.
- Multiple government organizations began investigations, and civil suits from the spill began almost immediately.
- The issue spread through both social media and the press, with consumers constantly trying to stay informed on the impact.
- Social media became a haven of discussion around the extent of the damage, images and video.
- Petitions, boycotts and uproar from animal advocate groups increased exponentially as complete coverage of BP's every move became transparent on the web.
- BP eventually won the *Consumerist* "Worst Company in America" contest in 2012.
- Legal action from both the government and the public continue to affect BP.

Relevant Media

Flickr currently has **over 25,000 photos** around the explosion and the effects of the spill

Deepwater Horizon Joint Info Center YouTube channel has **over 175 videos** and over **2.5M views** for its videos

Most Shared Sources:

BP Press Release
NY Times Article
CNN Article
Deepwater Horizon Joint Info Center YouTube Channel

BP Permanently Plagues Gulf of Mexico (2)

Brand Reaction:

- Issued multiple statements to the press around the issue.
- BP did not actively participate on social media during the crisis.
- Major U.S. government pages on Facebook, Twitter and YouTube were created to inform and update the public -- one of the largest efforts being run by RestoreTheGulf.gov.

Lessons Learned:

- Social media made an already horrific event significantly more impactful through real-time image, video and information-sharing.
- Social media and mainstream news both being sources for content amplifies the message across the web.

Relevant Media

Flickr currently has **over 25,000 photos** around the explosion and the effects of the spill

Deepwater Horizon Joint Info Center YouTube channel has **over 175 videos** and over **2.5M views** for its videos

Most Shared Sources:

BP Press Release
NY Times Article
CNN Article
Deepwater Horizon Joint Info Center YouTube Channel

"Janet" Dupes Exxon Mobil on Twitter

What Happened:

- In late July 2008, a user named "Janet" created the Twitter account @ExxonMobilCorp and tweeted about various subjects related to the company.
- The tweets were positive towards the company, but did reference controversial topics like the Valdez Oil Spill.
- For three days Exxon Mobil was unaware of the Twitter account until asked by the *Houston Chronicle*.
- Janet continued to tweet from the account days after Exxon was made aware of it.

Brand Reaction:

- They responded to reporters that the account was not them and that they currently aren't using blogs or social media to communicate.
- Exxon Mobil eventually created a corporate Twitter account.

Lessons Learned:

- It is important for a company to be aware of brand ambassadors and monitor any social media account that represents them.
- Fake corporate accounts can quickly gain followers, and require quick response.

Relevant Media

The account had over **400 followers** days after Exxon was made aware of it, yet they had not asked Twitter to remove it

Most Shared Sources:

Houston Chronicle Article
ZD Net Article
Jeremiah Owyang Blog Post

Exxon "Hates" Children

What Happened:

- On December 5, 2012 activist groups Oil Change International and The Other 98% launched a media campaign against Exxon with an advertisement stating "Exxon Hates Your Children."
- The video claims that Exxon is profiting off of destructive labor practices and therefore robbing future generations of a viable planet.
- "Exxon Hates Your Children" is raising funds to air the piece on television on channels to compete with American Petroleum Institute commercials. To date they have raised over $12,500 and have updated their website indicating it will air on TV soon.

Brand Reaction:

- On December 5, 2012 Exxon responded, calling the advertisement "offensive" to Exxon employees.

Lessons Learned:

- It's important to respond to activists in kin. In this instance Exxon looks as cold and defensive as they're made out to be. Responding with a video that illustrates Exxon's core values on their terms would have been more effective.

Relevant Media

Most Shared Sources:

Huffington Post Article

The Hill Article

Exxon Hates Your Children Website

Loud Sauce Fundraising

Redding Blog

Road Rage on Chrysler's Twitter (1)

What Happened:

- A tweet was posted on March 9, 2011 to the Chrysler Twitter page:

  "I find it ironic that Detroit is known as the #motorcity and yet no one here knows how to fucking drive."

- That same day, Chrysler removed the tweet and posted an apology on Twitter and on their blog.
- The post was captured by social media users and a few influential news outlets including *Mashable* and *Jalopnik* (partner site of *Gawker, Gizmodo, Lifehacker* and others)
- Chrysler's blog statement said the tweet was from an employee at one of their marketing firms, New Media Strategies.

Relevant Media

I find it ironic that Detroit is known as the #motorcity and yet no one here knows how to fucking drive

ChryslerAutos
Chrysler Autos

Most Shared Sources:

Mashable Article
Chrysler Blog
Post Apology
Jalopnik Article

Road Rage on Chrysler's Twitter (2)

Brand Reaction:

- Chrysler identified the employee as someone from a contracted marketing firm.
- The employee was immediately terminated.
- They ensured that they have taken the appropriate steps to keep this from happening again.

Lessons Learned:

- Controls need to be in place when employees (or contractors) are posting to official company web pages that will ensure the content isn't profane or offensive.
- Once a post is up on social media, images can be captured that will keep that story alive forever.
- Quietly remove the post before it can be reproduced and captured.

Relevant Media

I find it ironic that Detroit is known as the #motorcity and yet no one here knows how to fucking drive

ChryslerAutos
Chrysler Autos

Most Shared Sources:

Mashable Article

Chrysler Blog Post Apology

Jalopnik Article

General Motors Chars Cars

What Happened:

- On February 14, 2012 the National Highway Traffic Safety Administration announced an investigation into reports of fires in GM vehicles.
- On August 20, 2012, GM was forced to recall several lines of vehicles, affecting up to 1.5 million consumers.
- Faulty circuitry in doors reportedly caused 28 vehicle fires.

Brand Reaction:

- GM is voluntarily compensating individuals affected by the recall $100 to replace the faulty circuitry.
- GM has taken pains to make clear that the payment is for parts and labor, and is in no way a settlement.

Lessons Learned:

- Safety recalls will often cause consumers to worry, even if the issue is small.
- These recalls can be incredibly damaging to the brand's reputation.
- Companies must show that they will take complete fiscal responsibility -- making this visible across all marketing channels.

Relevant Media

6k tweets about GM recalls between February 2012 and September 2012

Most Shared Sources:

Forbes Article
Auto Blog
NY Times Article
GM Recall Website

ListenLogic
an AKUDA LABS Company

Jeep Grand Cherokee Fails "Moose Test"

What Happened:

- In early July, 2012 Teknikens Värld performed a "Moose Test" on the Jeep Grand Cherokee and it went up on two wheels.
- Teknikens Värld uploaded two videos that have been viewed over 900,000 times on YouTube.
- Chrysler released a statement decrying the test.
- *Consumer Reports* then had an issue during their testing for their famous car reviews.
- Soon after the *Consumer Reports* review was posted all over the web, Chrysler released a fix for the buggy software and recalibrated the stability control.

Brand Reaction:

- Chrysler initially released a statement stating that the exam was invalid and that the vehicle was overloaded.
- After *Consumer Reports* released their review, Chrysler was contacted and made the necessary repairs.

Lessons Learned:

- Videos on YouTube will stay up forever and be easily searchable once they have significant sharing.
- Identify influencers and work directly with them to identify all of the facts before issues arise that cannot be controlled on social media.
- Try to remove the videos before they go viral and are reproduced which significantly limits the containment options.

Relevant Media

Most Shared Sources:

Consumer Reports Article

Chrysler Blog Post

Reddit Thread

YouTube Video (1)

YouTube Video (2)

Honda Manager Fakes Facebook Review

What Happened:

- Over 2,000 comments were pouring into the Honda Crosstour Facebook page on September 2, 2009 after two "studio photos" were released. Commenters made clear that they didn't like the new design.
- Honda reported that 28 posts were deleted from the page for "profanity or inappropriate content".
- Eddie Okubo (Manager of Product Planning at Honda) posted a positive review on a Honda Facebook thread about their Crosstour.
- Commenter posted saying he worked for Honda followed by another comment posting a link to his LinkedIn profile.
- Between their dislike of the Crosstour design and the positive comment, Honda was left in a difficult position on Facebook, Twitter and many automotive blogs for the days following.

Brand Reaction:

- Honda removed his post in under 24 hours and released a statement stating that his post was removed because of a policy for associates requiring them to disclose their affiliation with Honda.
- They responded to criticism of the new design saying better pictures were on their way and that the initial ones were "like a bad yearbook photo or something".

Lessons Learned:

- To prevent "adding fuel to the fire," be sure to make clear to all employees the rules and risks involved with using social media.

Relevant Media

Most Shared Sources:

Auto Blog (Honda Employee Facebook Post)

Mashable Article (CrossTour Negative Comments)

Netflix Spin-Off Qwikster Gets Audiences All Wound Up (1)

What Happened:

- On July 12, 2011, Netflix announced price increases, which was not received well by subscribers.
- On September 18, 2011, Netflix announced via email they would be splitting up their business into streaming video and mail-order DVDs.
- The spin-off, Qwikster, was to be housed on a separate site, use a separate account and have the separate, but identical, price of $7.99. All of these features were unappealing to customers.
- The idea was universally panned, criticized and mocked by news outlets and influential personalities alike.
- By October 11, 2011, Netflix's stock had dropped 60%
- 800,000 subscribers left Netflix.

Relevant Media

75K tweets about Qwikster, and Netflix price hikes, between July 12, 2011 and December 2011

Most Shared Sources:

WSJ Article

The Oatmeal (Critical Comic)

Mashable Article

Twitter (Conan O'Brien)

Twitter (Funny Or Die)

Netflix Spin-Off Qwikster Gets Audiences All Wound Up (2)

Brand Reaction:

- On October 10, 2011 Netflix declared in a blog post that it would not split itself in two. The blog post was shared 2k times.
- On December 23, 2011 CEO Reed Hastings took a significant pay-cut, reducing his 2012 stock options from 3M to 1.5M.

Lessons Learned:

- Major corporate changes and decisions should include widespread statements and explanation, email isn't enough to inform consumers.
- Show consumers why the move is needed before they make their own judgement.

Relevant Media

75K tweets about Qwikster, and Netflix price hikes, between July 12, 2011 and December 2011

Most Shared Sources:

WSJ Article

The Oatmeal (Critical Comic)

Mashable Article

Twitter (Conan O'Brien)

Twitter (Funny Or Die)

SEC Charges Reed Hastings for Saying People Like Netflix (1)

What Happened:

- On December 5, 2012 Reed Hastings posted on his Facebook wall about Netflix subscribers amounting over 1 billion viewing hours:

    "Congrats to Ted Sarandos, and his amazing content licensing team. Netflix monthly viewing exceeded 1 billion hours for the first Time ever in June. When House of Cards and Arrested Development debut, we'll blow these records away. Keep going, Ted, we need even more!"

- Later that day, the SEC announced potential plans to file charges against Netflix or Hastings.
- The post was in reference to a milestone but disclosed information in a manner that was reportedly unequal to investors.

Relevant Media

Most Shared Sources:

<u>Reed Hastings Facebook Post</u>
<u>WSJ Article</u>
<u>NY Times Article</u>
<u>Mashable Article</u>

ListenLogic
an AKUDA LABS Company

SEC Charges Reed Hastings for Saying People Like Netflix (2)

Brand Reaction:

- Hastings later that day, commented about their use of social media:

  "We use blogging and social media, including Facebook, to communicate effectively with the public and our members"

Lessons Learned:

- The use of social media for official corporate communications is risky, as there are few written laws in this space.
- Prepare a press release rather than social media to be used before posting.
- Assume all posts on social media are like press releases and should follow that traditional convention to avoid legal implications of informally posting on social media.

Relevant Media

Most Shared Sources:

Reed Hastings Facebook Post

WSJ Article

NY Times Article

Mashable Article

ListenLogic
an AKUDA LABS Company

75 Million Playstation Network Accounts Compromised

What Happened:

- April 17, 2011, Playstation Network went down.
- Sony first admitted network was down on April 20th.
- Sony did not inform consumers that their personal information had been compromised until April 26th.
- Hackers got access to personal and financial data of at least 75 million accounts, including credit card information.
- Sony received widespread media criticism for their failure to disclose this information for a week.
- Sony was not able to restore service until May 14th 2011, 26 days later.

Relevant Media

Blog post by Sony admitting personal information breach was shared **100,000 times**

Most Shared Sources:

Upset PSN User (YouTube)

Wired Article

Time Article

New York Times Article

Sony Blog Post

Letter from U.S Senator

75 Million Playstation Network Accounts Compromised

Brand Reaction:

- Sony first admitted Playstation Network was down on the 20th.
- Waited a week to tell customers their data had been stolen.

Lessons Learned:

- Be aware of what your customers are saying about you, especially if it is negative.
- Do not let someone else tell the story about security and other sensitive issues.

Relevant Media

Blog post by Sony admitting personal information breach was shared **100,000 times**

Most Shared Sources:

Upset PSN User (YouTube)

Wired Article

Time Article

New York Times Article

Sony Blog Post

Letter from U.S Senator

Xbox Exec Mouths Off on Twitter

What Happened:

- Following Xbox announcing their new "always-on" Xbox 720, which will require constant internet access, there was significant backlash from the gaming community.
- On April 4, 2013, reacting to that feedback, Xbox Creative Director Adam Orth took to Twitter and berated fans that disagreed with Xbox's direction, telling those with less access to high quality Internet connection to "Deal With It".

Brand Reaction:

- Microsoft issued an apology several days after the Twitter tirade.
- Adam Orth is no longer with Microsoft, however, reports differ on whether he left or was dis-missed. His Twitter account has since been made private.

Lessons Learned:

- Damaging social media incidents can come from within, and from high-powered people.
- Having a social media policy governing employee's interactions with the Internet could help to avoid situations such as this.

Relevant Media

Most Shared Sources:

Game Informer

Major Nelson (Blog)

NBC News Article

TechCrunch Article

Forbes Article

EA Games Botches SimCity Launch, Wins Golden Poo

What Happened:

- EA launched the latest SimCity, which was soon found to be buggy, slow and prone to crashing.
- Users took to Amazon and rated the download 1/5 stars.
- EA Games was voted the Worst Company in America by Consumerist readers for the second year in a row, beating out companies like Bank of America and Wal-Mart. The prize for this contest is a golden poo statue.

Brand Reaction:

- EA games issued an apology, suspended 'non-critical' game features and boosted server capacity .
- Bug fixes and patches took over a month to roll out, and revealed even further issues with the UI and game functionality.
- EA acknowledged the Worst Company in America "win", and promised their customers they would improve.
- Weeks after the botched launch and Worst Company in America "win", EA closed their mobile division and laid off "60-70" permanent employees and "100" contracted workers.

Lessons Learned:

- When dealing with failed or flawed product launches, treating your customers tactfully is imperative.
- Failed product launches, and the ensuing digital fallout, can have lasting real-world effects on your company and brand; had EA handled their launch more skillfully they may never have lost the faith of their customers, who may not have voted against them in Consumerist's contest.

Relevant Media

Most Shared Sources:

BBC News Article

Huffington Post Article

The Next Web Article

TechCrunch Article

CNET Article

The Verge Article

Consumerist Article

ListenLogic
an AKUDA LABS Company

Linkedin Credentials Hack Affects Millions

What Happened:

- On June 6, 2012, around 6.5 million Linkedin passwords without the corresponding emails were leaked and published on a Russian hacker forum.
- Within hours of discovering the security breach, LinkedIn tweeted to update user's on the situation which was re-tweeted over 1,800 times.
- Several more updates were made via Twitter and made one update on Facebook
- LinkedIn published a blog post on June 9th explaining how to update and create stronger passwords.
- Reuters reported on June 20th that Katie Szpyrka of Illinois filed a $5 million suit against LinkedIn for violating promises to have better security in place. The case was reportedly difficult to prove and no resolution has been reported.
- Mashable reported on a June 29th blog post from LinkedIn that Twitter was not renewing their contract with LinkedIn. Speculation suggested that it may have been for several reasons, one being the security breach.

Brand Reaction:

- LinkedIn quickly posted on social media regarding the leaked passwords including their Facebook, Twitter, and blog.
- On June 12th, LinkedIn published a press release summarizing the steps that were taken to prevent breaches in the future and apologizing for the incident. LinkedIn did not publicly discuss the $5 million lawsuit.

Lessons Learned:

- LinkedIn is a different platform with access to larger amounts of personal data.
- Hacked LinkedIn accounts can often be much more damaging as hackers can see connections, personal data, and other critical data from company pages.

Relevant Media

Most Shared Sources:

LinkedIn Tweet

LinkedIn Facebook Post

LinkedIn Blog Post

LinkedIn Press Release

Reuters Article

Mashable Article

Google Fires Employee For Reddit Post (1)

What Happened:

- The middle of the last week in June, 2012 a Google employee took part in Chromebook training by Google.
- He then took to Reddit to promote the brand, mentioning that it will be sold at BestBuy.
- The next day, he received a call from Google saying that he was fired for violating the NDA that he had signed during the training period.
- The employee reposted on Reddit apologizing for disclosing the information and violating his NDA.
- His reposted Reddit thread has over 4,000 comments.
- The fired-employee took complete credit for the mistake and apologized.
- He then removed the original post with the image.

Relevant Media

Most Shared Sources:

Reddit Thread

GizModo Article

The Next Web Article

Google Fires Employee For Reddit Post (2)

Brand Reaction:

- Google fired the employee the next day after the initial Reddit thread was posted.
- They never responded to inquiries for a comment on the issue.

Lessons Learned:

- Posting images on the Web will allow screenshots and copies to be made instantaneously.
- In this case, like the image to the right, these images will be on the Web forever, even though the Reddit thread has been removed.
- Reddit has a different type of following that is very active on the Web, with threads that link to everything from images, to news to Twitter posts.

Relevant Media

Most Shared Sources:

Reddit Thread
GizModo Article
The Next Web Article

Dropbox Breach Breaks Trust

What Happened:

- On July 17, 2012, Dropbox users began getting e-mail spam as a result of a compromised Dropbox employee account that contained a list of client e-mail addresses.

Brand Reaction:

- Dropbox contacted all compromised accounts to help clients renew their passwords.
- On July 21 Dropbox blogged about the incident, outlining upcoming new security protocols.
- On August 26 Dropbox released a beta security update.
- On August 27 Dropbox released the security update to their entire user base.

Lessons Learned:

- As cloud-based storage becomes more common, companies must ensure protection of data.
- If data is not safe, trust is lost easily.

Relevant Media

20K Tweets about Dropbox security from July 17 to present

Most Shared Sources:

DropBox Blog

TechCrunch Article

Engadget Article

Ars Technica Article

CNET Article

GigaOM Article

Yahoo! Voices Hacked

What Happened:

- On July 11, 2012 hacker group D33DS stole ~450,000 usernames and passwords from the Yahoo! Voices application. Stolen e-mail credentials were from various e-mail services.

Brand Reaction:

- On July 12, 2012 Yahoo! issued a statement that the file stolen was 'older' and they were working to contact users with compromised credentials.
- Analysis of the breached information revealed a majority of easy, uncomplicated passwords at Yahoo!. Yahoo! received much criticism for not encouraging users to be more secure.
- Additional breach analysis showed that a minimally invasive hack was used, and that Yahoo! was not adequately protecting user data.

Lessons Learned:

- If data is not safe, trust is lost easily.
- Password-protection and security is not widely-known on the Web so it is dangerous when consumers don't know the extent of the damage from hacking.

Relevant Media

3.5K Tweets of articles about the issue

4.6K Facebook shares and likes of articles about the issue

Most Shared Sources:

Original Post (broken)

Trusted Sec Blog

Huffington Post Article

CNET Article

WSJ Article

The Next Web Article

ListenLogic
an AKUDA LABS Compa

Sexual Violence Pages on Facebook (1)

What Happened:

- In 2011, a Change.org petition called attention to rape pages that Facebook takes weeks to remove or denies the request all together.
- In August, Facebook was contacted by BBC and declined to take down the pages because they didn't want to censor.
- Advertisers then became concerned and had Facebook remove their advertising from these types of pages.
- Facebook still held their position after this corporate advertising move.
- The Change.org petition that snowballed in a few short months, was promoting tweeting and posting links to Facebook pages promoting rape and to use the hashtag #NotFunnyFacebook.
- Then on November 2, a day of action was organized by the petition, using the hashtag #NotFunnyFacebook to promote the issue further.

Relevant Media

Most Shared Sources:

AllFacebook Blog Entry

Ms. Magazine Article

BBC Article

Change.org Petition

Sexual Violence Pages on Facebook (2)

Brand Reaction:

- In August, Facebook commented:

  "It is very important to point out that what one person finds offensive another can find entertaining, just as telling a rude joke won't get you thrown out of your local pub, it won't get you thrown off Facebook"

- Facebook continues to hold their position on the matter.

Lessons Learned:

- Control the conversation before the issue can spread cross platforms (in this case it started as a petition, then spread to Facebook, Twitter and mainstream news).
- Do not provide the mainstream media with more incendiary information and topics to fuel the social media fire -- in this case censorship.

Relevant Media

Most Shared Sources:

AllFacebook Blog Entry

Ms. Magazine Article

BBC Article

Change.org Petition

Groupon and LivingSocial Offer Hurricane Sandy Deals Around NYC & the Jersey Shore (1)

What Happened:

- On October 30, 2012, a day after Hurricane Sandy passed through the New York City tri-state area, Groupon sent out targeted mobile and email ads to New Yorkers promoting a deal at a restaurant named Dans le Noir.

- Groupon also made headlines for offering a deal at Rustic L.E.S. in the Lower East Side neighborhood of Manhattan, an area without power after the storm.

- LivingSocial targeted locals with an ad for a "Seaside Sanctuary on Long Island" in Southold, NY, at a hotel that was closed, without power, and, at that time, had not yet set a date for re-opening.

- AdAge named Groupon's deal for Dans le Noir the "ultimate social media fail".

Relevant Media

Most Shared Sources:

The Atlantic Wire
AdAge Article
Huffington Post
Eater

Groupon and LivingSocial Offer Hurricane Sandy Deals Around NYC & the Jersey Shore (2)

Brand Reaction:

- Groupon responded by making their Northeast markets "opt-in only", and vendors' deals were postponed until they contacted Groupon.

- Groupon then launched a fundraising campaign for small business recovery.

- No official apologies for the offerings were made by Groupon or LivingSocial.

Lessons Learned:

- In the wake of a natural disaster, try to remove listings as quickly as possible for places that are closed as a result of it.

- Be wary of any language that can be perceived as insensitive or sarcastic with respect to the current situation. Ex:: "Dans le Noir", "Rustic" when no power.

Relevant Media

Most Shared Sources:

The Atlantic Wire

AdAge Article

Huffington Post

Eater

Verizon Fudges Fees, Succumbs to Customers

What Happened:

- December 29, 2011, Engadget reported a memo leaked from Verizon that stated a $2 convenience fee would be charged for one-time bill paying.
- Users posted on social media to express their opposition to this plan.

Brand Reaction:

- On December 30th, Verizon backed off from their plan and cancelled the fee.

Lessons Learned:

- Leaked information is far more tantalizing and aggravating than information given in a straight-forward manner.
- Fees around cable, Internet and phone attract much attention on the Web.
- Small issues like fees attract attention to other major issues in a company or industry.
- Highly potent issues can escalate quickly. Equally expedient response is key.

Relevant Media

~14k tweets about the fee between December 29, 2011 and December 31, 2011

~22k tweets about the fee between December 2011 and Jnauary 2012

~4k comments on the Huffington Post article below

Most Shared Sources:

Engadget Article (With leaked memo)
Droid LIfe Article
CNN Money Article
LA Times Article
Huffington Post Article

Samsung Bungles Blogger's Berlin Beat

What Happened:

* On September 2, 2012 The Next Web published a story about two Indian tech bloggers sent to Berlin, Germany for a conference.
* Bloggers agreed to go as reporters, not brand promoters.
* Samsung threatened to leave them in Berlin by cancelling their flights if they did not stay to promote their brand.
* Nokia covered the bloggers return fare and hotel arrangements, and is mentioned in most press regarding this story.
* Both bloggers blogged and tweeted about their treatment, causing others in the industry who had experienced similar treatment to discuss it as well.

Brand Reaction:

* On September 3, 2012 Samsung released a statement labeling the incident as a misunderstanding.
* Publically, Samsung acknowledged the incident, privately Samsung apologized for causing the bloggers 'undue hardship'. The bloggers released the private apology to the media.

Lessons Learned:

* Becoming a brand ambassador comes with the implicit assumption of positive portrayal on social media.
* Upsetting users with significant social media presence is extremely dangerous.

Relevant Media

Clinton Jeff @clintongeff

If you guys care about me as a person at all, you're going to want to read how Samsung abandoned me at IFA tnw.to/m3kc

7k Tweets about Samsungs hijacked bloggers from September 2, 2012 to present

2.3k Facebook shares

Most Shared Sources:

CNET Article

Telegraph Article

The Next Web Article

The Next Web Article (2)

Reddit Thread

Reddit Thread (2)

Samsung's "Sweatshops" Catch Heat

What Happened:

- On August 6, 2012, China Labor Watch released a report detailing the extreme conditions, underage workers, and unpaid hours occurring at eight Samsung factories in China .
- Issue received negative attention on technology blogs and social media.
- On September 10, 2012, China Labor Watch released another report claiming that Samsung uses discriminatory hiring practices, citing a recruitment poster seeking females without any communicable diseases.

Brand Reaction:

- On September 4, 2012 Samsung responded saying they had reviewed the situation and would start re-evaluating their labor practices in China, promising to sever ties with contractors who do not adapt to safer, legal, practices.
- Samsung denied the child labor allegations, claiming a 'zero tolerance' policy.

Lessons Learned:

- Consumers will lash back if they feel like their products are coming from places with poor working conditions.
- Labor and activist groups are very savvy when it comes to social media.

Relevant Media

6.5k tweets about Samsungs labor practices between August 2012 and September 2012

Most Shared Sources:

CLW Report
CLW Report (2)
CNET Article
The Verge Article
Huffington Post Article
Reuters Article

GLAAD Reneges on AT&T/T-Mobile Deal (1)

What Happened:

- On May 31, 2011, GLAAD wrote a letter to FCC Chairman Julius Genachowski supporting the AT&T/T-Mobile deal.
- Many gay rights blogs were outraged over the decision, including AMERICAblog and QUEERTY asking why a Gay Rights organization is making a strong case of support for a phone company merger.
- AMERICAblog helped to start the frenzy with an article on June 2, 2011.
- It was later learned that an ex-AT&T lobbyist, Troup Coronado, was one of GLAAD's board members, and that GLAAD had received money from AT&T in the past.
- National Gay & Lesbian Chamber of Commerce President Justin Nelson said that the original letter draft supporting the deal was supposed to garner additional gay rights groups support before being sent.
- The President resigned after it was revealed that he sent a letter to the FCC in January 2010, opposing their Net Neutrality rules, which AT&T opposes.
- At the end of June 2011, additional members resigned after the controversy.

Relevant Media

Most Shared Sources:

Letter to FCC
AMERICAblog
Politico Article
ARS Technica
Article

GLAAD Reneges on AT&T/T-Mobile Deal (2)

Brand Reaction:

- President Barrios and 6 board members resigned at the end of June.
- The organization withdrew its support of the deal.
- Other Gay Rights groups came out in support of the idea of supporting the deal, but did not support that specific letter to the FCC.

Lessons Learned:

- Highly controversial issues spark hostile and politicized debates on social media and blogs.
- Track blogs and influencers that are outspoken about their opposition to major issues and may bring attention to concerns that may wish to be kept quiet.
- Control the message and clarify any stance on a major Internet-based issue that will spark debate on blogs, forums, and social media.

Relevant Media

Most Shared Sources:

Letter to FCC
AMERICAblog
Politico Article
ARS Technica Article

Nokia Lumia 920: Caught in a Lie (1)

What Happened:

- On September 5, 2012 Nokia released an advertisement for their new flagship phone, the Lumia 920.
- Nokia failed to include "screen images simulated" note, making viewers think the video was filmed by the phone.
- The Verge dissected the video and noticed a camera crew in the background.
- Nokia apologized on their blog for the ad and released the video that was shot with the Lumia 920.
- On social media influential news/blogs criticized Nokia for starting off their flagship brand promotion with false advertising.

Relevant Media

Original footage on YouTube has over **1M views**

Most Shared Sources:

The Verge Article
The Verge Article (Apology)
YouTube Video Fake Ad
YouTube Video Real Nokia Ad
Nokia Blog Apology

Nokia Lumia 920: Caught in a Lie (2)

Brand Reaction:

- Nokia agreed the ad was misleading and stated that it was meant to show what they'd be doing with OIS:

  > ""produced a video that simulates what we will be able to deliver with OIS... [it was] never the company's intention to deceive anyone"

- They updated their blog with an apology and note that the 920 did not shoot the advertisement.
- They added a note to the fake ad stating that it was not produced with the phone.

Lessons Learned:

- As media spreads online, it becomes more and more difficult to pull down.
- Don't lie to early adopters in the tech world.
- Be honest and forward on social media if it is a mistake, allowing the company to control the facts.

Relevant Media

Original footage on YouTube has over **1M views**

Most Shared Sources:

The Verge Article

The Verge Article (Apology)

YouTube Video Fake Ad

YouTube Video Real Nokia Ad

Nokia Blog Apology

Apple's iOS 6 Release Flattened by Maps Fail (1)

What Happened:

- On Wednesday September 19, 2012, Apple released the latest operating system, iOS 6, for the iPhone and iPad with new features including a new Maps app that replaced the previous app developed by Google.
- It was a highly anticipated app, but within hours of its release users began complaining about errors and a lack of features including transit directions.
- A Tumblr, "Amazing iOS 6 Maps", began collecting images of the errors including flattened buildings (instead of 3D), mislabeled major cities, erased entire towns.
- The next day popular technology blogs began writing about the complaints and highlighting some of the "best" images collected on the Tumblr account.
- A parody Twitter account, @iOS6maps, was created briefly before it was shut down by Twitter.

Relevant Media

Over 80,000 posts about Apple Maps between 9/19-9/21

Over 15,000 posts linked to the Tumblr account between 9/19-9/21

Most Shared Sources:

Amazing iOS 6 Maps Tumblr

Mashable ArticleAnil Dash Blog Post

Apple's iOS 6 Release Flattened by Maps Fail (2)

Brand Reaction:

- Apple responded to the complaints saying they "appreciate all of the customer feedback and are working hard to make the customer experience even better."
- On Sept. 20, Apple competitor, Nokia, posted on their blog touting their map offering while subtly pointing out that they built and distributed their own mapping app unlike their competitors.

Lessons Learned:

- Even a company as widely loved as Apple is not immune to criticism on social media.
- Users had high expectations for the new maps and when there are obvious errors and inconsistencies, Apple should have been prepared for there to be backlash.

Relevant Media

Over 80,000 posts about Apple Maps between 9/19-9/21

Over 15,000 posts linked to the Tumblr account between 9/19-9/21

Most Shared Sources:

Amazing iOS 6 Maps Tumblr
Mashable ArticleAnil Dash Blog Post

McDonalds Botches Billboard Translation

What Happened:

- Around the end of August, put up a McDonalds billboard in a Hmong neighborhood of St. Paul, MN.
- On September 1, media coverage picked up criticism from Hmong people who said that the billboard was offensive and incorrect.
- The overall language and writing on the billboard (meant to say "Coffee gets you up, breakfast gets you going.") is ultimately confusing to the Hmong people.
- After significant media and Web coverage, McDonald's Midwest Region's marketing director, Gregg Miskiel responded to the Associated Press.

Relevant Media

Most Shared Sources:

Pioneer Press Article (Original Source)

AdWeek Article

Consumerist Article

Huffington Post Article

McDonalds Botches Billboard Translation

Brand Reaction:

- Louis Henry, operator of 8 McDonalds in the Twin Cities area commented that he was confident in the overall reach of the advertisement.
- Henry also said that he hopes to see rotating Hmong advertisements every few weeks, having gotten the idea from a fellow Twin Cities operator and ad agency, Arnold MPG.
- Two weeks after the incident, McDonald's Midwest Region marketing director apologized in an Associated Press article.
- Marketing director Miskiel also stated that they will correct the errors and re-post the billboards soon.

Lessons Learned:

- Consult a linguist/translator before marketing in a different language so the ad isn't offensive.
- With social media's prevalence, all content is global, so a small incident can reach any number of people.

Relevant Media

Most Shared Sources:

Pioneer Press Article (Original Source)

AdWeek Article

Consumerist Article

Huffington Post Article

AT&T Charges Millions of Dollars for Roaming Data

What Happened:

- On August 20, 2012, Ryan Kearney tweeted a breakdown of AT&T roaming charges for SMS messages claiming that a Gigabyte of messages costs ~ $3.3 million. Soon after posting it, AT&T replied to his tweet attempting to correct him but deleted it shortly after.
- On the same day, Kearney blogged about the interaction and reworked his calculations. The post was shared over 160 times and commented on over 60 times.
- Kearney also posted it on Reddit. The post gained nearly 1,000 comments.
- Many posts discussed the technical aspects of the calculations.

Brand Reaction:

- AT&T responded to Kearney in a tweet trying to correct him but shortly after, deleting the tweet.

Lessons Learned:

- Be sure to have tight control of social media accounts. Responses should be well-timed and executed to be effective.

Relevant Media

Most Shared Sources:

Ryan Kearney Tweet

Ryan Kearney Blog Post

Ryan Kearney Reddit Thread

Gizmodo Article

AntiSec Hacks FBI, Leaks Apple's Juicy ID's

What Happened:

- On September 3, 2012 hacking group AntiSec tweeted an announcement claiming to have accessed an FBI laptop and stolen a file containing the UDID's of 12 million Apple device users.
- In order to prove the breach 1,000,001 of those UDID's were released for the public to download, followed by vague threats regarding the status of the other 10,999,999 UDID's.

Brand Reaction:

- On September 4, 2012 the FBI denied having the UDID's in the first place via a formal press release and Twitter.
- On September 5, 2012 Apple denied, in an interview, providing UDID's to the FBI, and the UDID's would be replaced with more updated technology.

Lessons Learned:

- Trading personal data and government intervention behind consumers backs is risky.
- Getting out in front of the leak, rather than basic denial, will often help repair the public opinion around a brand's attempt to control the issue.

Relevant Media

11.6k Tweets about Anonymous and UDID's

5k Facebook posts about Anonymous and UDID's

690k views of the original post on Pastebin

Most Shared Sources:

Original Post - Pastebin

AnonymousIRC Tweet

FBI Twitter Response

Apple Response - AllThingsD

Gizmodo Article

Mashable Article

ListenLogic
an AKUDA LABS Company

AT&T Loses Throttling Small-Claims Case

What Happened:

- In December 2011, Michael Spaccarelli could not satisfactorily stream video to his AT&T smartphone despite his unlimited data plan, and received a text message telling him his data usage was in the top 5% of AT&T users in his area.
- On February 24, 2012 Spaccarelli was awarded $850 as a reimbursement for the data he paid for but could not use after taking AT&T to small claims court.

Brand Reaction:

- On March 1, 2012 AT&T released a web site explaining their new data restrictions and educational materials regarding 'smart' data usage.

Lessons Learned:

- Small issues can often shed light on much more major issues (this led to unlimited data plans/family share plans).
- Prepare contingency plans for potentially high-profile legal issues.

Relevant Media

600k Tweets about AT&T throttling unlimited data plans between September 2011 and April 2012

Most Shared Sources:

NY Times Article

Mashable Article

The Consumerist Article

Businessweek

Reddit Thread

Change.org Petition

Lovers Quarrel: DirecTV vs. Viacom

What Happened:

- On July 10th 2012, DirecTV informed their customers via Facebook that Viacom executives sent them a letter stating that if they don't come to an agreement by midnight that day, DirecTV must remove Viacom channels.
- All Viacom channels were blacked out from DirecTV customers for the next 10 days until the companies came to an agreement on July 20th.

Brand Reaction:

- During the 10 day dispute both companies used Twitter, Facebook, YouTube, and other sites to defend their case.
- Viacom's Twitter channels promoted the hashtag, #WhenDirecTVDrops .
- DirecTV promoted the hashtag, #DIRECTVHasMyBack.
- Stars of shows on Viacom channels used social media to support Viacom's position.
- Both companies created dedicated websites explaining their side of the dispute.

Lessons Learned:

- While both companies used social media to reach out to customers, there was no clear winner in the eyes of customers. Many blamed both companies for being greedy.
- The number of different things being said on social media was huge and without a dedicated listening solution it would be impossible for either company to find the posts/issues that were really being discussed by customers.

Relevant Media

There were over **350,000 posts** across various social media outlets on July 10-11

DirecTV's Facebook post has over 4,000 comments

Most Shared Sources:

DirecTV Facebook Post

Mashable Article

CNN Money Article

#TakeMyMoneyHBO Organically Goes Viral (1)

What Happened:

- On Tuesday June 5, Jake Caputo (blogger and website developer) developed a website, TakeMyMoneyHBO.com, asking how much people would be willing to pay for standalone HBO service.
- He then tweeted a link to the website and then posted on Reddit.
- Within 2 hours, his hashtag, #takemymoneyhbo had been posted over 1,500 times on Twitter.
- Within the first 3 hours, US News & World Report and TechCrunch reached out to him on Twitter.
- Within the next 12 hours, TechCrunch, The Next Web, Business Insider, AdWeek and Digital Trends released articles on the issue.
- On Wednesday June 6, responded via Twitter referencing the TechCrunch article providing an analysis of why HBO doesn't have plans to implement this plan:

  "Love the love for HBO. Keep it up. For now @RyanLawler @TechCrunch has it right: http://itsh.bo/JLtSFE #takemymoneyHBO"

Relevant Media

Hashtag: Posted **over 7k times in 17 hrs**

Website: Over 160k users voted on TakeMyMoneyHBO.com

Most Shared Sources:

TakeMyMoneyHBO Website

TechCrunch Article

HBO Twitter Response

#TakeMyMoneyHBO Organically Goes Viral (2)

Brand Reaction:

- HBO responded 1 day after the campaign started, linking to Ryan Lawler's article on TechCrunch describing why HBO isn't interested in this distribution method.

Lessons Learned:

- Mainstream media helps to propel hashtags and social media based trends.
- Once the media becomes involved in something start on Twitter, Facebook, etc., it is difficult to stop, or even get in front of it with a comment.
- HBO waited until the news explained why it wasn't viable right now, rather than issuing a statement immediately after the hashtag went viral.
- Engage users when the idea is new and fresh, on the platform on which it began, to help with perspective and the company's side of an issue.

Relevant Media

Hashtag: Posted **over 7k times in 17 hrs**

Website: Over 160k users voted on TakeMyMoneyHBO.com

Most Shared Sources:

TakeMyMoneyHBO Website
TechCrunch Article
HBO Twitter Response

AMC takes on Dish In Contract Renewal (1)

What Happened:

- For the month of June, 2012 Dish and AMC were in a heated contract dispute.
- On July 1, 2012 Dish officially dropped AMC Network channels after no resolution was agreed upon before the blackout date.
- Dish has stood behind the blackout saying that AMC is asking too much.
- AMC said that Dish is holding a grudge for a lawsuit over a channel VOOM HD from years before.
- Each company started attacking the other in advertising, both on the Web and on television.
- AMC started marketing campaigns and promotions to entice Dish subscribers to switch so that they could keep the channels.
- DirecTV and AMC each tried to start hashtags after the blackout started (ex. #DirectvHasMyBack).
- Social media erupted with a variety of hashtags, people commenting about switching providers immediately.

Relevant Media

Most Shared Sources:

Reuters Article

New York Times Article

Entertainment Weekly Article

Gawker Article

AMC takes on Dish In Contract Renewal (2)

Brand Reaction:

- Dish and AMC each provided statements to the press and on their websites, with Dish CEO Charlie Ergen giving comment about cost.
- They began attacking each other in the press, on their websites and on TV.
- AMC started keepamc.com to help consumers switch to other providers.
- They also offered a free online live stream of the Breaking Bad season premier to Dish subscribers.
- Then they started a viral marketing campaign by releasing actors portraying zombies (to promote *The Walking Dead*) in NYC.

Lessons Learned:

- Trying to use social media as a weapon can backfire as DirecTV's Twitter hashtags led to the creation of other hashtags by users on the Web that could not be controlled.
- Taking away content from consumers and only giving them a reason that it costs too much won't suffice when they know that they pay a lot for access to THAT specific content.

Relevant Media

Most Shared Sources:

Reuters Article

New York Times Article

Entertainment Weekly Article

Gawker Article

Foxconn Employees Threaten Mass Suicide

What Happened:

- In January of 2012, 300 Foxconn workers threatened to commit mass suicide for undisclosed reasons. One worker was reportedly promised a raise.
- Employees were told they can quit with compensation or stay without a raise.
- The New York Times and other influential news sources reported on the issue and many posted on Twitter, Facebook, YouTube and a Reddit thread that quickly gained over 2,000 comments.

Brand Reaction:

- Foxconn resolved the issue after an 8 hour stand off once the Mayor of Wuhan convinced them to get down and Foxconn gave them raises but not after 45 quit.
- Microsoft released a statement acknowledging their partnership and trust in Foxconn to continue to evolve their process and work relationships.
- Statement also said that they are "committed to---the safe and ethical treatment of people who build [their] products".

Lessons Learned:

- Consumers will lash back if they feel like their products are coming from places with poor working conditions (Nike boycotts over clothing).
- This almost always draws attention from consumer groups and news.

Relevant Media

Most Shared Sources:

New York Times Article

Atlantic Wire Article

Reddit Thread

162

Apple Story Rots The Barrel for Public Radio

What Happened:

- On January 6, 2012 *This American Life* aired an excerpt of Mike Daisey's performance, which claims Apple had knowledge of Foxconn's labor conditions.
- On March 16, 2012 *This American Life* retracted the show, as it most of Daisey's account was found to be false.
- On March 16, 2012, Daisey also released a statement apologizing only for not being more clear about the difference between theatre and journalism.

Brand Reaction:

- On January 13, 2012 Apple released a statement regarding the podcast, as well as a never-before-seen list of global components suppliers.
- The statement also promised to enact a comprehensive supply chain audit.
- On January 13, 2012 Foxconn raised the wages of their workers between 16-20%.

Lessons Learned:

- Child labor concerns must immediately be addressed by a company, even if just false allegations.

Relevant Media

880,000 downloads of the original TAL Podcast

250,000 times the original TAL podcast was streamed

100,000 times the monologue has been downloaded

Most Shared Sources:

This American Life - Show Transcript

This American Life - Retraction

The Agony and Ecstasy of Steve Jobs - Monologue

Apple Response to This American Life

The Verge Article

Tech Crunch Article

ListenLogic
an AKUDA LABS Company

Fox News Airs Suicide on Live TV

What Happened:

- On September 28, 2012 Fox News live broadcast a high-speed car chase which concluded with the driver killing himself. Fox News was unable to prevent the suicide from airing, even though the footage was on a five-second delay.
- Videos of the segment were immediately uploaded to the internet and several dozen articles were published commenting on the issue.

Brand Reaction:

- Immediately after an abrupt commercial break anchor Shepard Smith profusely and emotionally apologized for the footage that should not have been aired.
- The evening after the segment aired Fox News released a statement apologizing and blaming human error.

Lessons Learned:

- Dealing with accidents decisively and quickly may not help to minimize the issue, but will help to set the tone for how your brand is perceived going forward.

Relevant Media

Collected YouTube videos had more than **3,246,435 views**

11,200 Tweets

13,000 Facebook "Likes" and "Shares"

Most Shared Sources:

Huffington Post Article

ABC News Video

NPR Article

New York Times Article

Fox News Statement

Associated Press' Twitter Hacked, Tanks DOW Jones Index

What Happened:

- April 23, 2013 the Associated Press Twitter account was compromised by the Syrian Electronic Army.
- The offending tweet claimed that there had been two explosions at the White House and that Barack Obama had been injured, the tweet was reposted 3,146 times.
- As a result of the tweet, the Dow Jones Industrial Average and the S&P 500 were affected, both markets "plummeting" in the minutes following the post.
- Other AP accounts were also hacked, posting tweets referencing Syria.
- It was later learned that the hack followed a sophisticated phishing e-mail sent to AP staffers the same day.

Relevant Media

Most Shared Sources:

Huffington Post Article

BBC News Article

Mashable Article

TechCrunch Article

NY Post Article

Associated Press' Twitter Hacked, Tanks DOW Jones Index

Brand Reaction:

- Within minutes the AP began responding from AP verified Twitter accounts, including the hacked one, and via Facebook, telling readers "please do not respond to news posted there in the last 20 minutes".
- The account has been suspend, The AP are investigating security issues with Twitter.
- AP security investigated the phishing e-mail and warned staffers about phishing attempts.

Lessons Learned:

- Handling emergent situations immediately is imperative.
- The AP dealt with this situation swiftly and transparently, apprising the public of their continuing steps to resolve the issue.

Relevant Media

Most Shared Sources:

Huffington Post Article
BBC News Article
Mashable Article
TechCrunch Article
NY Post Article

ESPN Slurs Racism at Jeremy Lin (1)

What Happened:

- On Feb. 17, 2012, the Knicks winning streak supported by bench-player Jeremy Lin, was snapped by the New Orleans Hornets.
- Hours later, ESPN released an article on the loss titled, "Chink In The Armor", which resulted in Twitpics and Instagram photos all over the Web.
- On Saturday Feb. 18, ESPN issued an apology on their Media Zone website and also posted on Twitter:

   ESPN.com Editor-in-Chief Rob King: "There's no defense for the indefensible. All we can offer are our apologies, sincere though incalculably inadequate."

- The Asian American Journalists Association said in a letter to ESPN that this shouldn't have been posted to begin with and retracting the story wasn't enough.

Relevant Media

Most Shared Sources:

Fox News Article

Huffington Post Article

ESPN Director of Comm Tweet

ESPN Slurs Racism at Jeremy Lin (2)

Brand Reaction:

- ESPN removed the offensive headline, changed the title of the story.
- They apologized on their Media Zone website and on Twitter, stating that it was only available on the Web, and was not aired on their broadcast channel.
- They fired an editor allegedly responsible for the incident and indicated that they would review their process.

Lessons Learned:

- Anything posted on the Web can be captured in video and images that will be difficult or impossible to takedown after the fact.
- Find the source of the issue and quietly take care of it before too many photos can be reproduced that will be spread across the Web forever.
- Monitor and track discussion around a brand-damaging incident with insensitive material and use social media to interact with upset readers/viewers.

Relevant Media

Most Shared Sources:

Fox News Article

Huffington Post Article

ESPN Director of Comm Tweet

Chiefs Insult Fan on Twitter

What Happened:

- On September 10, 2012 around 6 PM, Kansas City Chiefs fan Travis Wright @teedubya, posted a negative message about the Chiefs.
- Around 8 PM that night, Travis Wright received a message from the Kansas City Chiefs official Twitter account saying "Your choice to be a fan."
- On September 11th, 2012, Travis Wright posted an image of this message on Reddit, and the story went viral.
- The Chiefs posted an apology on their Twitter account later on September 11th.
- By the morning of September 12th, the story received national news coverage.
- By the afternoon of September 12, Travis Wright had appeared on several local TV and radio shows to discuss the issue.

Brand Reaction:

- Chiefs then blocked user via Twitter.
- Chiefs later apologized via Twitter, and released statement admitting fault for incident.

Lessons Learned:

- Assume anything sent/posted on any social media volume can be shared with the world at any time.
- Never insult customers or fans on social media.
- See how influential people are before you interact with them.

Relevant Media

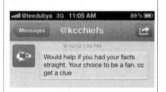

Over 5,000 posts around Reddit Thread

Most Shared Sources:

Original Post

Image of 'private' Message

Reddit Thread by Fan

Mashable Article

Yahoo! Sports Article

NBC Sports Article

NFL Replacement Referees: Awful Officials (1)

What Happened:

- In June 2012, NFL referee's went on strike. Replacement referees were called in and underperformed in every respect.
- Specific events during high-stakes games were highlighted as examples of extremely bad, and occasionally dangerous, calls:

  > *9/24/2012 Packers-Seahawks controversial touchdown call*

  > *9/23/2012 Houston player loses an earlobe due to a violent hit, which was not penalized*

  > *9/23/2012 Oakland player loses consciousness for 10 minutes, is concussed and hospitalized after a violent hit, which was not penalized*

- Poor calls caused complications for betting pools, fantasy leagues and resulted in fines for players, coaches and teams.
- This strike led to unfavorable comparisons to the concurrent labor protests of Chicago teachers and Chinese Foxconn employees.
- Players, politicians, and fans protested the referees online.

Relevant Media

424K Tweets about the bad call at the Packers-Seahawks game

1.3M YouTube views of the bad call at the Packers-Seahawks game

Most Shared Sources:

TJ Lang Tweet

Barack Obama Tweet

The Daily Show Clip

Washington Post Article

Packers-Seahawks Videos

Huffington Post Article

NFL Replacement Referees: Awful Officials (2)

Brand Reaction:

- The NFL escalated resolving the issue with the Referee's union.
- On September 27, 2012 an agreeement was reached between the NFL and the NFL Referees Association, 48 hours after the Packers-Seahawks game.

Lessons Learned:

- Controversial moments, like the replacement referees calls, live on infinitely on social media.

Relevant Media

424K Tweets about the bad call at the Packers-Seahawks game

1.3M YouTube views of the bad call at the Packers-Seahawks game

Most Shared Sources:

TJ Lang Tweet

Barack Obama Tweet

The Daily Show Clip

Washington Post Article

Packers-Seahawks Videos

Huffington Post Article

ListenLogic
an AKUDA LABS Company

Jeff Jarvis Blogs about Dell Customer Service

What Happened:

- In June 2005, Blogger Jeff Jarvis shared a story on his personal blog about a Dell laptop that was having issues and Dell's poor customer service in response.
- His blog post received many comments from others with similar stories of bad customer service from Dell.
- Jarvis continued blogging about Dell and his experience, he bought a Mac, and sent an Open Letter to Michael Dell suggesting that the company pay attention to blogs.

Brand Reaction:

- Initially Dell had no response.
- By April 2006, Dell began to respond to bloggers complaints.
- In July 2006, Dell started their own blog, Direct2Dell.

Lessons Learned:

- Even in 2006 before Twitter, companies could not afford to ignore their customers.
- Now it is even more important to realize they must reach out to customers on social media, and not hope they go away.
- It took Dell a while to react to this crisis but they did, and now understand the value in monitoring and responding.

Relevant Media

"**Thousands** of frustrated consumers eventually commented on and linked to my blog, saying, 'I agree.'"
-Jeff Jarvis in BusinessWeek

Most Shared Sources:

Jeff Jarvis Blog Post

BusinessWeek Article

Microsoft Cashes in on Japan Earthquake

What Happened:

- On March 12, 2011, @Bing tweeted that for every retweet they would give $1 to victims of the earthquake in Japan up to $100,000.
- While many people did simply retweet the message without complaint, others began to criticize Microsoft for trying to take advantage of the disaster.
- 2 hours after the initial tweet, influential comedian Michael Ian Black tweeted @Bing telling them to stop using the tragedy as a marketing opportunity.

Brand Reaction:

- 7 hours after their initial tweet @Bing tweeted an apology and said they donated $100K.

Lessons Learned:

- Waiting 7 hours to apologize allowed time for the criticism to build and influencers like Michael Ian Black to comment on it.
- Within the first hour Microsoft could have seen the conversation turning negative and apologize then instead of waiting.
- Companies need to be very careful when tweeting about current events, especially tragedies.
- Wording can be the difference between people praising a company for goodwill or criticizing them for making it a marketing opportunity.

Relevant Media

How you can #SupportJapan - http://binged.it/fEh7iT. For every retweet, @bing will give $1 to Japan quake victims, up to $100K.
about 7 hours ago via CoTweet
Retweeted by 100+ people

 bing
Bing

Michael Ian Black had over **1.5 million** followers at the time of his tweet

His tweet was retweeted almost **1,000 times**

Bing's apology tweet was retweeted only **550 times**

Most Shared Sources:

@Bing's Original Tweet

@Bing's Apology Tweet

@michaelianblack's Tweet

VentureBeat Article

Reebok Promotes Promiscuity (1)

What Happened:

- In March 2012, a Reebok print ad in Germany Gym had the slogan: "Cheat on your girlfriend, not on your workout."
- On March 17, images of the ad began appearing on Twitter, including a tweet from a trainer on NBC's *The Biggest Loser*.
- On March 18, a YouTube video was uploaded which has gone on to reach 100,000 views.
- On March 19, CheaterVille.com sent an email to Reebok saying they had received over 5,000 emails linking to pictures of the ad, and that they said "we will start informing our millions of followers to boycott Reebok until the ad is removed and a public apology is given".

Relevant Media

Most Shared Sources:

Brett Hoebel
Twitter Post
YouTube Video
CheaterVille
Email
Huffington Post
Article

Reebok Promotes Promiscuity (2)

Brand Reaction:

- On March 20, Reebok issued an apology, and removed the ads saying it was not a global campaign.

Lessons Learned:

- Social media can turn an issue that occurred in another country into a domestic issue.
- A controversial story can go national, or international, quicker than ever, and companies must be vigilant in their monitoring of social media.

Relevant Media

Most Shared Sources:

Brett Hoebel
Twitter Post
YouTube Video
CheaterVille
Email
Huffington Post
Article

Maytag Insults Influential Mother

What Happened:

- In 2009, Heather Armstrong purchased a new Maytag washer that required repair multiple times.
- Throughout 2009 Heather then called Maytag and told a customer service representative and supervisor of her problems and her influence on Twitter.
- CSR and supervisor said they could not help and her influence did not matter.
- Heather tweeted repeatedly about the negative service she received.
- Maytag/Whirlpool executive then reached out to Heather and solved the problem quickly.
- Bosch, a competitor gave Heather a free washer that she donated to a worthwhile charity.

Brand Reaction:

- Whirlpool representative reached out via Twitter to Armstrong and got a repairman to fix the broken washing machine.
- Whirlpool competitor Bosch her a free washing machine via Twitter, which she donated.

Lessons Learned:

- Companies and service representatives should take influence into account when reaching out to customers online.

Relevant Media

So that you may not have to suffer like we have: DO NOT EVER BUY A MAYTAG. I repeat: OUR MAYTAG EXPERIENCE HAS BEEN A NIGHTMARE.

1:19 PM Aug 26th from Tweetie

 dooce
Heather B. Armstrong

Blog post received **5,000 comments and shares**

Heather had over **1 million Twitter followers** and over **300,000 readers** on her Blog

Most Shared Sources:

Dooce.com Blog Post

Forbes Article

ListenLogic
an AKUDA LABS Comp

Target Accused of Subversively Targeting Women

What Happened:

- On December 3, 2007, a Flickr photo was posted of a Target billboard in Times Square that was viewed nearly 24,000 times and gained over 60 favorites and comments.
- In January of 2008, the founder of the blog ShapingYouth.org, Amy Jussel, sent an email to Target criticizing a billboard that she viewed as inappropriate.
- Target responded saying they don't participate with non-traditional media outlets.
- The response drove Jussel, Steve Hall and others to blog about the ad.

Brand Reaction:

- Target responded to the NY Times saying they do not work with bloggers currently but they are reviewing the policy and may adjust it. Spokesperson continued by saying, "This practice is in place to allow us to focus on publications that reach our core guest".

Lessons Learned:

- Not recognizing blogs as a media outlet is an antiquated policy.
- Bloggers, Tweeters, etc... have the power to bring as much, if not more, negative publicity to them now than traditional media does.

Relevant Media

Flickr photo caption:

"suggestivemuch?"

Nearly 24,000 views

Most Shared Sources:

Original Flickr photo

ShapingYouth.org Blog

Adrants Blog

NY Times Article

ListenLogic
an AKUDA LABS Company

Walmart's PR Firm Pays for Fake Blog (1)

What Happened:

- On Sept. 27, 2006 a new blog "Wal-Marting Across America" began detailing the travels of Jim and Laura in an RV traveling to Walmart's across the country.
- The blog only included stories and pictures of Walmart employees that really loved where they worked.
- People began to question openly on the Internet whether the blog was real.
- On Oct. 9, 2006, BusinessWeek revealed that the blog, RV, gas, etc.. was paid for by Working Families for Walmart, an organization created by Walmart's PR firm, Edelman.
- The BusinessWeek story quickly spread throughout the blogosphere and generated a lot of negative comments.

Relevant Media

Most Shared Sources:

BusinessWeek Article

CNN Money Article

Walmart's PR Firm Pays for Fake Blog (2)

Brand Reaction:

- Edelman's CEO admitted that they were responsible for failing to be transparent about the blog and said Edelman is responsible for the error, not Walmart.

Lessons Learned:

- It's important that brands be transparent on social media: it's only a matter of time before someone digs deep enough to find the truth.
- Companies must be careful when trusting an agency to run their social media presence, as the risks are greater and you lose control if you aren't involved.

Relevant Media

Most Shared Sources:

BusinessWeek Article

CNN Money Article

Walmart's Black Friday Fight Club

What Happened:

- On November 10, 2011, Walmart released a statement outlining efforts to avoid the seasonal violence that had come to be associated with it's stores.
- On November 24, 2011 (Thanksgiving Day) Walmart opened their doors and made some deals available at 10pm.
- On November 25, 2011 (Black Friday) there were over 20 incidents in nine Walmart stores.
- Help responded, but many Walmarts remained open during the events and after despite the violence.
- Violence, and often its response, was documented by witnesses cell phones and posted via Twitter, Facebook and YouTube.

Brand Reaction:

- Walmart has not issued a statement regarding this years violence.

Lessons Learned:

- Consumers aren't "normal shoppers" on Black Friday, preparations must be made for extraordinary situations.
- Make the safety protocol known before shopping commences.

Relevant Media

Cell phone and news footage videos have over **3.2M Youtube views** since November 25, 2011

40k Facebook shares

3.4k Tweets

7k Comments on article and videos

Most Shared Sources:

Walmart Press Release

LA Times (Local)

Digitriad Article

ABC News Article

Detroit Free Press Article (Summary of Events)

ListenLogi
an AKUDA LABS Comp

Main Market for Kenneth Cole: Egyptian Protests

What Happened:

- On February 3, 2011, Kenneth Cole tweeted from his company's official account saying:

  > "Millions are in uproar in #Cairo. Rumor is they heard our new spring collection is now available online at http://bit.ly/KCairo - KC"

- The tweet occurred as the protests in Egypt were escalating, and many Twitter users immediately criticized the company calling the tweet "awful", "offensive", "evil", etc...
- Multiple fake "Kenneth Cole" Twitter accounts were created making fun of the tweet and saying other offensive things.

Brand Reaction:

- An hour after the original post, Kenneth Cole tweeted again apologizing for the tweet.
- Cole also posted an apology on his Facebook page.
- Later that day they took down the original tweet.

Lessons Learned:

- Controversial hashtags and trends should never be used for promotions, as customers will not only see right through it, but share the incident quickly and the reaction will be overwhelmingly negative.

Relevant Media

According to the Associated Press, @KennethCole's Twitter account gained **over 3,000 followers** within hours of the tweet

Most Shared Sources:

CNN Money Article

Mashable Article

OMM Hates Ellen, Boycotts JC Penney

What Happened:

- On January 25, 2012 Ellen DeGeneres was chosen to by JC Penney as a spokesperson.
- Immediately the special interest group, One Million Moms started a campaign to get JC Penney to drop her as a spokesperson.
- On Friday February 3, JC Penney released a statement of support for Ellen.
- GLAAD then immediately began a support campaign for Ellen on Facebook and via petition.
- On February 8, Ellen brought up OMM on an episode of her show:
  "They wanted to get me fired, and I'm proud and happy to say that JCPenney stuck by their decision to make me their spokesperson, which is great news for me because I also need some new crew socks."

Brand Reaction:

- JC Penney supported their decision of Ellen as a spokesperson and conveyed that support via social media and the press.

Lessons Learned:

- Remember that activism by powerful groups like One Million Moms will bring much negative attention.
- Do not back down from the group because of negative press on social media and rather point out why the candidate is a good fit.

Relevant Media

Most Shared Sources:

Huffington Post Article (Ellen's Comments)
Reuters Article

Adidas Enslaves Customers With Shackle Shoes (1)

What Happened:

- In January, images of the shoe appeared in the SneakerNews blog.
- On June 14, 2012 Adidas used Facebook to promote the Roundhouse Mid "Handcuff" shoe:

  > *"Tighten up your style with the JS Roundhouse Mids, dropping in August. Got a sneaker game so hot you lock your kicks to your ankles?"*

- Comments on Facebook were both negative and positive but focused on slavery.
- Civil rights groups asked the NBA commissioner to intercede in the issue.
- During the day of June 18, Adidas responded and later that evening, Adidas provided a second response that they will withdraw the shoe.
- The designer tweeted that it was never his intention to reference slavery.

Relevant Media

Most Shared Sources:

CNN Article
Yahoo! Article

Adidas Enslaves Customers With Shackle Shoes (2)

Brand Reaction:

Relevant Media

- Adidas provided an initial response:

  "...The design of the JS Roundhouse Mid is nothing more than the designer Jeremy Scott's outrageous and unique take on fashion and has nothing to do with slavery...Any suggestion that this is linked to slavery is untruthful."

Most Shared Sources:

CNN Article

Yahoo! Article

- A second response later on June 18th:

  "Since the shoe debuted on our Facebook page ahead of its market release in August, Adidas has received both favorable and critical feedback. We apologize if people are offended by the design and we are withdrawing our plans to make them available in the marketplace."

Lessons Learned:

- Understanding consumer sentiment and discussion is critical through the entire product development lifecycle.

Political Deathmatch: QVC vs. Jane Fonda (1)

What Happened:

- On July 16, 2011, Jane Fonda was contacted by QVC that her appearance had been cancelled after numerous calls from people threatening to boycott the show because of Fonda's opposition to the Vietnam War.
- That same day, Fonda posted on her blog that her appearance on QVC to promote a new book had been cancelled because of her political comments about the Vietnam War.
- Later that day, she also posted twice on Facebook thanking her fans for their support after her cancellation on QVC.
- QVC did not notify viewers that it had cancelled the appearance.
- Mainstream news including the Associated Press wrote about Fonda's posts and the story went viral.
- In a later book expo, Fonda argued about QVC nixing the appearance.
- Comments on social media supported Fonda but said she was quick to blame the "well funded and organized political extremist groups".

Relevant Media

Her blog and Facebook posts have been **shared over 3,200 times**

Most Shared Sources:

Jane Fonda Blog Post

Jane Fonda Facebook Post 1

Jane Fonda Facebook Post 2

WSJ Article

Huffington Post Article (AP)

Political Deathmatch: QVC vs. Jane Fonda (2)

Brand Reaction:

- QVC released a statement saying that it had cancelled the appearance but did not give a specific reason.
- They did not inform their viewers that her appearance was cancelled.

Lessons Learned:

- Strong social media involvement by an influential celebrity garnered much attention for an issue that may have otherwise gone basically unnoticed.
- Using multiple mediums expands the reach and viewer numbers of each post, increasing the likelihood that the issue will be picked up by mainstream media.
- In this case, involvement and support from fans caused the mainstream media (WSJ, Associated Press, etc.) to spread this story from social media onto the mainstream Web.

Relevant Media

Her blog and Facebook posts have been **shared over 3,200 times**

Most Shared Sources:

Jane Fonda Blog Post

Jane Fonda Facebook Post 1

Jane Fonda Facebook Post 2

WSJ Article

Huffington Post Article (AP)

Generic Pen Picks Kryptonite Locks (1)

What Happened:

Relevant Media

- On September 12, 2004, a post on BikeForums.net described how to pick bike locks requiring a tubular key with a pen.
- Over 1,200 more posts were made on the thread and several posted videos demonstrating different models.
- In the next few days, several influential news sources reported on the issue including New York Times, Los Angeles Times, Wired, and Engadget. All causing exponential awareness across the Internet.
- YouTube videos continue to be posted. One from October 2009 has gained over 500,000 views; another video from October 2008 has gained over 325,000. A total of over 850 comments were left between the two.

Most Shared Sources:

BikeForums.net Forum
NY Times Article
Wired Article
YouTube Video
YouTube Video

Generic Pen Picks Kryptonite Locks (2)

Brand Reaction:

- In a September 16th statement made to the New York Times, Kryptonite said they were aware of the issue and were "moving quickly" to replace existing locks and to provide new locking mechanisms for new lines of locks. The spokesperson reportedly stressed that other manufacturers share the same weaknesses.
- Eligible locks sold after September 2002 were exchanged at no cost.
- Spokesperson for Kryptonite's parent company, Ingersoll-Rand, also commented saying that the security flaw was "not a Kryptonite concern...this is an issue with some tubular cylinders, not all." They went on to say that earnings won't be affected as Kryptonite sales were less than 1% of the company's over $10 billion in annual sales.

Lessons Learned:

- This type of widespread security risk can cost a company more than capital. Regardless of how little it may affect the bottom line, customer loyalty is at the forefront of successful corporations in the digital age.

Relevant Media

Most Shared Sources:

BikeForums.net Forum
NY Times Article
Wired Article
YouTube Video
YouTube Video

Too Much Pressure Explodes Some Toilets (1)

What Happened:

- On September 26, 2011, a formal report was made to the U.S. Consumer Product Safety Commission (CSPC) via Safeproducts.gov detailing an injury caused by a Flushmate III Pressure Assisted Flushing System that had exploded.
- The product was sold at retail locations including Lowe's, Home Depot, and several well known toilet manufacturers.
- On June 21, 2012, a warning was issued by CSPC and Health Canada on the same day the toilet was voluntarily recalled by Flushmate.
- 304 exploded toilets have been reported as of August 2012 in addition to 14 laceration or impact injuries.
- A lawsuit was filed in Las Vegas in early August 2012 against Flushmate and its parent company Sloan Valve Co.
- One YouTube video was posted of an exploded toilet that has been viewed over 3,000 times since April 22, 2012.

Relevant Media

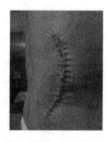

Most Shared Sources:

Safeproducts.gov Report

U.S. CSPC Press Release

Health Canada Press Release

Flushmate Recall Site

YouTube Video

Too Much Pressure Explodes Some Toilets (2)

Brand Reaction:

- Flushmate voluntarily recalled over 2.3 million U.S. unites and over 9,000 Canadian units.
- Flushmate created a page on their site that people can use to find out if their toilet is being recalled.
- Affected users are provided with a repair kit, which some claim is ineffectual.

Lessons Learned:

- Angry consumers considering legal action are empowered by social media.
- Next steps after a recall now require frequent communication with both the media and consumers.

Relevant Media

Most Shared Sources:

Safeproducts.gov Report

U.S. CSPC Press Release

Health Canada Press Release

Flushmate Recall Site

YouTube Video

ListenLogic
an AKUDA LABS Company

Walmart Contest Hijacking Sends Pitbull to Alaska (1)

What Happened:

- In early July, 2012 Walmart and Sheets Energy Strips started a Facebook campaign for each store to gather as many likes as possible on the page.
- The store that had the most likes by July 15, 2012 would receive a visit from Pitbull.
- Two writers, David Thorpe (writer for the Boston Phoenix) and Joe Hendren of the site SomethingAwful.com decided to convince Web users to use the hashtag #exile Pitbull to promote the Kodiak, Alaska Walmart.
- A Reddit thread was also started to help them in their hijacking.
- If the Kodiak Walmart won, Pitbull would need to take a trip to the northernmost Walmart in North America.
- In a matter of days, Kodiak garnered over 60,000 likes (more than 10x its population) and eventually won the contest.
- Pitbull posted on Twitter that he would gladly go wherever for his fans and even invited the hijacker, David Thorpe to join.

Relevant Media

Over 3,000 posts around #exilepitbull hashtag

Most Shared Sources:

Mashable Article

Huffington Post Article (Associated Press)

Reddit Thread

ListenLogic
an AKUDA LABS Company

Walmart Contest Hijacking Sends Pitbull to Alaska (2)

Brand Reaction:

- Walmart and Pitbull positively responded on Facebook and Twitter that he would in fact be visiting the Alaskan city.
- The responses came around July 15, 2012.

Lessons Learned:

- It is easy to hijack a social media contest that requires voting.
- Hashtags help issues on one social platform spread to another very quickly (in this case what started on Facebook spread to Twitter and Reddit in a matter of days).

Relevant Media

Over 3,000 posts around #exilepitbull hashtag

Most Shared Sources:

Mashable Article

Huffington Post Article (Associated Press)

Reddit Thread

Ralph Lauren Outsources Olympic Uniforms

What Happened:

- In early July, Ralph Lauren provided the U.S. Olympic team uniforms, however, they were made in China.
- Congress was infuriated, with multiple influential Representatives and Senators commenting publicly.
- The USOC spokesman Patrick Sandusky publicly supported Ralph Lauren, stating that the U.S. is one of a few nations whose Olympic team is privately funded.
- Sandusky then took to Twitter to again support Ralph Lauren.
- An 800M track Olympian also Tweeted against Ralph Lauren's production in China.

Brand Reaction:

- The USOC spokesman supported Ralph Lauren to the news and again on Twitter.
- Ralph Lauren reportedly declined to comment on the matter.

Lessons Learned:

- Participation in very public events can bring up new controversies.
- Companies must identify the "hot-button issue" they're tied to or risk getting caught off guard.

Relevant Media

Most Shared Sources:

ESPN Article

Huffington Post Article

Nike Olympics Tee Sparks Sexism Debate

What Happened:

- At the start of the Olympics, Nike (an official sponsor) released their t-shirt that read, "Gold Digging".
- Major blogs and social media users took to the Web to protest the shirt, stating that it is sexist and degrades the Olympic womens' efforts at the games.
- The t-shirts were widely distributed for sale and one shop, World Soccer Shop, even listed a description: "We aren't saying they're gold diggers - we're just saying they're out for the gold! What's wrong with that?"
- Other users and commenters on the Web stated that they found the shirt to be amusing.

Brand Reaction:

- Nike originally declined to comment on the issue.
- They contacted Shine from Yahoo! roughly 1 week later:

  "Nike has consistently supported female athletes and the position they enjoy as positive role models. The T-shirt uses a phrase in an ironicWay that is relevant given it was released just as the world focused on the success of female athletes."

Lessons Learned:

- Potentially controversial steps for a brand (products, ads, etc.) should be introduced with trial balloons.

Relevant Media

Most Shared Sources:

Yahoo! Article

Jezebel Article

Toys 'R' Us Cursing Doll Remains on Shelves

What Happened:

- In mid-November, 2011 a few parents emailed complaints to Toys 'R' Us complaining about a swearing doll.
- They then took the story to local news outlets in various cities around the country.
- The news reached out to Toys 'R' Us, but they originally declined to comment on the issue.
- Conversation picked up enough around the issue that eventually the issue was covered on *Good Morning America* and Huffington Post.
- Toys 'R' Us eventually commented a few days later when contacted by ABCNews.com.

Brand Reaction:

- Toys 'R' Us initially declined to comment or respond to the complaints that they received on their website.
- A Toys 'R' Us spokeswoman Jennifer Albano said there are no plans to discontinue the doll trio or pull them from shelves.

Lessons Learned:

- Deal directly with mothers before they take to the Web to voice their argument, where activist groups may throw gasoline on the fire.

Relevant Media

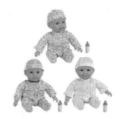

Most Shared Sources:

ABC News Article

Huffington Post Article

Celeb Boutique Uses Massacre Hashtag to Sell the "Aurora" Dress

What Happened:

- Twitter hashtag #Aurora was trending shortly after the shooting in an Aurora theater on July 20, 2012. Over 260,000 tweets have used the hashtag.
- Celeb Boutique tweeted, "#Aurora is trending, clearly about our Kim K inspired dress ;)"
- The Kim Kardashian dress is named the "Aurora".
- Nearly 600 people responded to the tweet within the first hour before being deleted.
- In the hours following, Celeb Boutique apologized in a series of 5 tweets which garnered over 1,000 retweets and 'favorites'.
- Storify posted about the incident has been viewed over 10,000 times.

Brand Reaction:

- Brand posted multiple apologies via Twitter, claiming ignorance of the event and deleted the offensive post.

Lessons Learned:

- Research hashtags and how they're used before implementing one for marketing/sales on social media.

Relevant Media

Most Shared Sources:

Mashable Article
Huffington Post Article
Storify Post

Ikea Removes Women from Their Saudi Catalog

What Happened:

- On October 1, 2012 Metro Sweden revealed that Ikea had adjusted their catalog for Saudi Arabia by removing most images of women.
- On October 2, 2012 the Tumblr blog "I(KEA) GOT 99 PROBLEMS BUT A BITCH AINT ONE!" launched, featuring diptych of images of women replaced with Ikea products. The blog hosts over 105 such images.

Brand Reaction:

- On October 1, 2012 Ikea released a statement, claiming to tailor content according to the receiving culture:

  "We are now reviewing our routines to safeguard a correct content presentation from a values point-of-view in the different versions of the Ikea catalogue worldwide"

Lessons Learned:

- Even with the best of intentions (like tailoring content to the receiving culture) dealing with something as complex as global gender politics should be carefully considered from every angle.

Relevant Media

Most Shared Sources:

Metro - Sweden
Ikeafiles Parody Tumblr
The Lede
The New York Times Article
Huffington Post Article
The Guardian Article
Wall Street Journal Video
LA Times Article
NPR Article
CNN Article
NBC News Article
BBC News Article
Mashable Article

ListenLogic
an AKUDA LABS Company

Model Behavior: Hollister's South Korean Embarrassment (1)

What Happened:

- On August 30, 2012 Hollister launched their first South Korean retail store and flew American models to attend the opening.
- During their visit models posted racially insensitive photos and derogatory comments to social media, in addition to other disrespectful behavior, such as flipping off Korean photographers and reporters at press events.
- On September 7, 2012 koreaBANG published a lengthy and critical blog entry with screenshots of the offensive behavior.
- On September 11, 2012 congressman Michael Yaki accused Hollister's parent company, Abercrombie & Fitch, of failing in their efforts to diversify and promoting a culture of racism, referring to a 2003 class-action lawsuit.

Most Shared Sources:

Korea Bang Article

Huffington Post Article

Angry Asian Blog

Oh No They DIdn't! Blog

Styleite Blog

Daily Mail Article

The Gloss Blog

Jezebel Article

Model Behavior: Hollister's South Korean Embarrassment (2)

Brand Reaction:

- On September 9, 2012 Hollister issued an apology via Facebook which read:

  ""In summary, the company terminated the couple of associates involved. On behalf of our more than 80,000 associates around the world who cherish our core values and our culture of diversity and inclusion, we sincerely apologize for the offense caused by these unauthorized, ill-considered actions."

- The apology has since been removed.

Lessons Learned:

- Clear policies are necessary when a large number of employees can represent your brand

Relevant Media

Most Shared Sources:

Korea Bang Article

Huffington Post Article

Angry Asian Blog

Oh No They Didn't! Blog

Styleite Blog

Daily Mail Article

The Gloss Blog

Jezebel Article

ListenLogic
an AKUDA LABS Company

Urban Outfitters "Juan at Walmart" Shirt Angers Latinos

What Happened:

- On December 29, 2012 Latinos Unidos of SUNY Fredonia tweeted a picture of a workshirt with patches that read "Juan" and "Walmart". The tweet asked "is it racist?"
- On December 29, 2012 the issue was picked up by Latino Rebels, an activist and social justice group that focuses on Latin American interests.
- Latino Rebels uses the hashtag #nomames, which is mexican slang for "f*ck off", to describe issues they find particularly ridiculous and offensive and runs a regular "No Mames" feature.

Brand Reaction:

- On January 2, 2013 Urban Outfitters "Retail Strategy" Team responded to the Latino Rebels, claiming that the shirt is a vintage one-of-a-kind item in their inventory, along with other similar workshirts.

Lessons Learned:

- Patrons and customers can, and will, take pictures of your products. Regardless of the reality of the situation, if the slightest offense can be read into a product it's likely others will be offended as well.
- Involvement with media savvy activists is to be avoided at all times.

Relevant Media

Most Shared Sources:

Original Tweet

Facebook - Latino Rebels

Latino Rebels Blog Entry #1

Latino Rebels Blog Entry #2

Huffington Post Article

Bank of America's Debit Regret (1)

What Happened:

- On July 21, 2010 the Durbin Amendment to the Consumer Protection Act was signed into law. This regulation cap would prevent banks from collect-ing fees from merchants when cus-tomers use their debit cards.
- In January 2012 Bank of America intended to launch a $5/month fee designed to help BoA avoid losing money because of the Durbin Amendment. This was announced through mainstream media sources.
- Customers became outraged, and threatened to cancel their accounts because of the fee. Reactions were tweeted, and a November 5 Bank Transfer Day was arranged via Facebook.
- The issue added another spark to the Occupy Wall St. movement over corporate greed.

Relevant Media

Over 500K tweets

The Bank Transfer Day Facebook page has 57k likes, and remains active presently

Most Shared Sources:

Reuters Article

NY Times (Cancellation)

Salon Article

YouTube (Move Your Money Project)

ABC News Article (Bank Transfer Day)

The Stir - Cafe Mom Blog

Facebook - Bank Transfer Day

ListenLogic
an AKUDA LABS Company

Bank of America's Debit Regret (2)

Brand Reaction:

- Bank of America cancelled the planned fee, as did Wells Fargo and JP Morgan who were planning similar fees.

Lessons Learned:

- Show consumers the reasoning for unpopular decisions, before officially announcing a rollout.
- When a company is under significant public pressure to prove they are socially responsible, trying to gain more money from customers can be misconstrued.

Relevant Media

Over 500K tweets

The Bank Transfer Day Facebook page has 57k likes, and remains active presently

Most Shared Sources:

Reuters Article

NY Times (Cancellation)

Salon Article

YouTube (Move Your Money Project)

ABC News Article (Bank Transfer Day)

The Stir - Cafe Mom Blog

Facebook - Bank Transfer Day

ListenLogic
an AKUDA LABS Company

Progressive Allegedly Defends Killer

What Happened:

- In August of 2012, Progressive was accused of defending the driver who killed Kaitlynn Fisher in a car accident.
- Kaitlynn's brother wrote a Tumblr post on Aug. 13th that was then reposted by over 12,000 users and shared ~13,000 times on Twitter.
- Over 21,000 other tweets mention the issue.
- The Consumerist picked up the story and published a total of 4 articles around the issue along with Reddit threads and other news sources.

Brand Reaction:

- Progressive released a statement clarifying that they did not represent the driver who killed Fisher.
- According to The Consumerist, Progressive was a defendant in the case.
- After the Fisher's won their case, Progressive worked with them to fulfill their contractual obligations.

Lessons Learned:

- A statement after-the-fact will seem like catch-up.
- A company needs to provide proof of innocence, offer a gesture to counter the allegations.

Relevant Media

Most Shared Sources:

Original Tumblr Post

Consumerist Article

Reddit Thread (Incident)

Reddit Thread (Backlash)

Red Cross Drunken Tweet

What Happened:

- On February 15, 2011, a Red Cross employee tweeted a personal tweet from the wrong account. The employee accidentally used the Red Cross Twitter account when she was expressing her excitement about Dogfish Head's beer, Midas Touch.
- Dogfish responded to the tweet positively by turning it into a blood drive for Red Cross. Many Dogfish distributors participated in what was called, "blood-for-beer" offers.
- An hour after the tweet was made, it was deleted and the social media director attempted to call the employee followed by two tweets responding to the mistake.
- By 4 PM on February 16th, the employee commented on her own Twitter account and blamed the mistake on hootsuite.

Brand Reaction:

- Red Cross responded via Twitter telling followers saying, "We've deleted the rogue tweet but rest assured the Red Cross is sober and we've confiscated the keys."
- On February 16, the Red Cross posted on their blog thanking supporters for using the incident to increase donations. The blog post was shared nearly 16,000 times including Twitter, Facebook, and Google+ in addition to others. Post also gained over 150 comments.

Lessons Learned:

- Employees using official company accounts need to be careful when using 3rd party apps for posting.

Relevant Media

American Red Cross
@RedCross

Ryan found two more 4 bottle packs of Dogfish Head's Midas Touch beer.... when we drink we do it right #gettngslizzerd

Most Shared Sources:

RedCross Initial Response Tweet

Dogfish Head #gettingslizzered Initiative

Gloria Huang (Personal) Tweet

Red Cross Blog Post

CNN Money Article

Mashable Article

ListenLogic
an AKUDA LABS Compan

Peyton Manning's Massive Tip Gets Waiter Dismissed

What Happened:

- On March 7, 2012 a waiter posted an image of a 50% tip from NFL star Peyton Manning.

Brand Reaction:

- The Angus Barn fired waiter "Jon", because Manning's full name and the last four digits of his credit card were revealed.
- Restaurant owner stressed her desire to have discretion.
- The restaurant owner reportedly called Manning to apologize.

Lessons Learned:

- Photographs have staying power, and these days most employees will have a camera in their cell phone.
- Companies must control the social media policies of its staff, and back up those policies with swift and decisive consequences.

Relevant Media

3.7K Reddit comments

Most Shared Sources:

Original - Sweater Punch Article
Reddit Thread (1)
Reddit Thread (2)
NBC17 Video
The Star Article
Eater Article
USA Today Article
Food Beast Blog

Chapter 4 - Managing Social Risk

Risk management – and the intelligence that enables it – is huge business. There are lots of wealthy risk management consultants. Companies must understand the risks that surround their business models; they must also understand the risks that threaten their industries. They are willing to pay for this intelligence. So should you.

As discussed in Chapter 2, risk committees are expected to oversee the risk assessment process. A company's lines of business are responsible for defining, implementing and managing risk strategies. As presented in Chapter 3, there are at least 100 ways for companies to lose their social way.

Again, when referencing the drivers for deploying a real-time *cyber monitoring* strategy, risk committees most commonly reference the following:

- *Business interruption due to a cyber attack on their network*

- *Business interruption due to supplier and/or customer cyber disruptions*

- *Employment-related risk due to the use of social media*

- *Reputational damage to the organization via social media*

- *Denial of service attack or virus on the organization's servers*

- *Theft/loss of the organizations assets/intellectual property*

- *Infringing others' intellectual property*

- *Privacy violations/Data breach of customer records*

But, as also discussed, awareness of the risks around social media is relatively low, focused almost exclusively on improper employee usage of social networks and tweets, blogs and posts made by disgruntled customers. Executives seem to understand that there is *some* risk involved in social media; yet this risk has not been well-defined. Governance structures to monitor compliance and manage social risks are therefore still in the early stages.

This chapter looks at the range of issues and opportunities surrounding the management of risks traceable to social media. Chapter 3 describes what happens when social media becomes the unfortunate venue for corporate events and conditions. Companies must continuously gather and interpret social business intelligence to better understand the world in which they live as well as the threats to which they're vulnerable.

Avoiding #Fail is about understanding, planning for and, ultimately, managing multiple forms of social risks. Social risks happen slowly *and* fast; they're "local" *and* "viral." Companies need to allocate resources to *social risk intelligence* and *social risk management*. The threat is real – and sometimes even self-inflicted.

Social Risk Management

Social risk management (SRM) is multi-dimensional. Surrounding the SRM process are of course the flavors of risk that should drive SRM planning:

- *Operational Risk* – how exposed is a company is to the disruption of it its operations

- *Reputational Risk* – how protected a company's brands and corporate reputation actually are

- *Compliance Risk* – how effectively a company complies with laws and regulations

So how should Boards and senior management teams respond?

Directors are expected to opine and advise on corporate strategy, the business model and risk management, using their personal experience, industry best practices and information furnished by the corporation's management team. Unless there are specific issues regarding the trustworthiness of management, the Board is best positioned to review social media analytics when the information is provided to them *through management* – which is the preferred source: business units have every reason to listen to social media and to manage potential problems. Boards should require SRM; business units should *implement* BRM (and report to the Board on a quarterly basis).

Why haven't more Boards of Directors required management develop a process for collecting, analyzing and responding to social media intelligence? Do boards actually know what questions to ask? Can boards distinguish between a good system for monitoring social media and a bad one? Probably not, but Boards should task management to pursue a workable SRM strategy.

An important aspect of board responsibility is to monitor organizational reputation. How is this currently done? Should overall sentiment derived from social media sources be a primary input for social risk analysis? Which social media metrics should be presented and which excluded? Where do the responsibilities of the Board end and those of management begin?

More than 80% of Companies with USD 1Billion or more have board policies on risk oversight and management (Aon Risk Solutions, Global Risk Management Survey, 2011).

According to a Deloitte study, 58% of executives believe that reputational risk associated with social media should be a board room issue. But only 17% of companies currently have a program in place to capture this data (Deloitte, Social Media Report 2012: http://www.deloitte.com/view/en_AU/au/services/specialist_serv ices/innovation/social-media-report/index.htm).

Boards should require management to target specific social risks and organize to identify and manage these risks. Senior management teams should implement, fund and continuously improve social risk intelligence and social risk management policies and procedures.

There are two broad categories of social risk that SRM strategy and tactics should address:

- *Risks identified through social business intelligence*

- *Risks as a result of social media activity*

SRM Requirements

Here's a list of requirements that SRM demands be addressed through whatever technology/social listening and management vendor you select. At the very least, that vendor (or perhaps your internal SRM team) should be able to do the following:

- *Provide situational awareness through alert, mapping and analysis of open-source (social and other) actionable intelligence*

- *Provide an open-source intelligence collection capability through a robust open- source platform that has the flexibility to change search parameters and geo-locate searches based on breaking events, crisis or emerging threats*

- *Be capable of rapidly assembling and providing critical open source information and intelligence that will allow companies to vet, identify, and geo-locate breaking events, incidents and emerging threats, as well as the capacity to allow companies to retain control of cached and real-time proprietary data, the ability to share with selected partners, and ultimately enhancing coordination, synchronized-awareness and synergy at the operational level*

- *Map stakeholder involvement in order to support enhanced strategic, operational and tactical information for improved decision-making*

Vendors (or, again, perhaps your internal SRM team) should be able to ask-and-answer the following kinds of questions:

- *Is there a good chance that this situation will, if left unattended, escalate in intensity? What are the indicators that support the analysis?*

- *Might the situation foster unwanted attention by outsiders, such as the news media or a regulatory agency? What precedent data can be leveraged to better understand the drivers of event participation?*

- *Is it likely that the situation might interfere with normal business operations in some manner? If so, how?*

- *Whether or not the published content is accurate, does it have the potential to negatively impact our reputation with our stakeholders? How much and to what extent?*

- *How is it going to affect our bottom-line? What is the quantitative impact of a social crisis?*

SRM Capabilities

As suggested in Chapter 2, companies (through their vendors or internal teams) therefore need to be able to do the following:

- *Provide warning*

- *Detect specific, credible threats to monitor adversarial situations*

- *Identify bad actors (activists, saboteurs) and analyze their movements, their expressed timelines, and potential adverse actions that the client can take*

- *Predict likely developments in the situation or future actions taken by bad actors (by conducting trend, pattern, association, and timeline analysis)*

- *Detect instances of deception in intent or action by bad actors for the explicit purpose of misleading the brand or relevant law enforcement*

- *Develop domain and influencer assessments for the purpose of strategic communications (typically in response to an event or crisis)*

- *Develop pattern-of-life matrices to support strategic planning and risk response*

- *Detect potential threats*

- *Develop threat profiles*

- *Outline possible courses-of-action*

- *Determine timeframe for action by actors*

- *Identify and develop a tactical picture of the event*

- *Develop intelligence products for counter-measures*

Companies need to chart their *Standing Intelligence Issues* (i.e. boycotts, physical threats, and petitions), and identify emerging topics or indicators of pending adverse events. For example: *unauthorized, tell-all by celebrity reveals off-label use of a product.*

Companies also need a *Dashboard* that provides real-time analytics on-demand accessible to keep the risk team apprised of developing situations.

The essential capabilities include the ability to track ("listen"), profile and pro-act/re-act. Put another way, SRM capabilities require the ability to describe, explain, predict and prescribe events and conditions as discovered via social media.

Companies must also understand the nature of *Social Influence.* "Influence" on the Internet today is often preemptively judged by such distorted metrics as number of Facebook friends or Twitter followers, a user's Klout score, or simply the number of times they post. Often disregarded in the analysis of true influence, are metrics that require significantly more detailed research, such as *who* the followers or friends are and where those networks lead. It is evident that hundreds of tools preach that they have a simple way to justify why they believe Kim Kardashian is more influential than Craig Moffett, but their flawed rationale results in extremely misleading assumptions. A few of the tools – like Klout[1] and PeerIndex[2] – are popular, but only skim the surface when identifying a user's true influence.

The ideal understanding of influence on the Internet needs to be more carefully dissected and vetted before tools like Klout, PostRank or Twiangulate can boast about offering an all-in-one breakdown of a user on social media. Often overlooked are such simple metrics as:

- *Who are someone's followers and how does a user posting to their 50 followers reach millions of people around the globe?[3]*

- *Does someone have a 2nd, 3rd, 4th, Nth degree connection that leads them to someone influential?*

- *On how many platforms is the user active?*

- *Are they content creators or viewers? Active or dormant? Creative-style media (photos/video) or repurposing content (links/retweets) that is already on the Web?*

- *Do they use mainstream sites (Facebook, Twitter, LinkedIn, etc.) or is primary communication through smaller topic-specific sources (blogs/forums/etc.)*

---

[1] According to their site (http://klout.com/corp/klout_score), Klout uses over "400 signals from seven different networks. We process this data on a daily basis to generate updates to your Klout Score. The majority of the signals used to calculate the Klout Score are derived from combinations of attributes, such as the ratio of reactions you generate compared to the amount of content you share."

[2] According to their site (http://about.peerindex.com/), PeerIndex "measures interactions across the web to help you understand your impact in social media" as well as, "online social interactions to determine your impact in social media and beyond."

[3] See the Preface for the chart regarding influential users in the Aetna CEO vs. Arijit Guha case.

However influential a user is labeled (Justin Bieber vs. Barack Obama vs. Jack Welch), it is often the interaction between them and other users that will ultimately determine the true reach of content posted on the Internet.

Let's look at the range of Social Influencers that social risk managers should understand and track:

Creators → *Arijit Guha*

- *Post original content (posts, videos, photos, articles, etc.)*

- *Often relied on for new content that other users read (e.g., comedians, activists)*

- *Use the other types of influencers to truly reach more people, groups, discussions, etc.*

Connectors[4] → *Sourav Guha, "Little John," Jen Wang*

- *Use additional platforms to spread the message*

- *Bring additional followings into the discussion – cross-platform integration*

- *Add own twist to original content to add value (hashtags, @, links, etc.)*

Extenders → *Michael Moore*

- *Often have extensive networks in sheer numbers (Charlie Sheen has over 8 million followers on Twitter)*

- *Post content to the eyes of many more users – especially with blog/forum use*

Unexplainables → *Beth Kanter – "social media expert" (@kanter - 400k followers)*

---

[4] Malcolm Gladwell, 2002. *The Tipping Point.* New York, NY: Little, Brown & Company.

- *Strong follower #s, but isn't always obvious why so many*

- *Potential for the "black market" of social media – spam, fake users, etc.*

- *Users can purchase "bot" or "spam" followers on Twitter*

Amplifiers → Colon Cancer Alliance, Center for Public Integrity

- *Repost, "favorite," "like" content but rarely generate their own*

- *May broadcast to a new network via another platform*

- *Often is related to articles, videos and celebrities postings*

How do *Social Influencers* behave? What tools do they use? Here's a list that social risk managers must understand:

- *Hashtags (# can backfire if used maliciously, subversively)*

- *Timing of the posting (time of day, pre-event, etc.)*

- *Post to walls, profiles of news, known influencers, etc.*

- *Target columnists, writers, and bloggers for major news to attract their attention without getting lost in every other post targeting the outlet itself (e.g., @waltmossberg vs. @wsj)*

- *Post to active users involved in that issue/topic, even without prior connection*

- *Use of false friends/followers to boost perceived influence*

- *Be creative with media (GIFs, videos, images, etc.)*

- *Avoid highly controversial topics that others may be concerned about reposting*

- *Don't post so often that an overall message is diluted*

- *Videos for YouTube and Vimeo*

- *Short + concise posts, links and images for Twitter*

- *More detailed content and images for Facebook, etc.*

- *Full image spreads for Pinterest and Flickr*

- *Professional and concise for LinkedIn ...*

SRM Strategy & Tactics

There are a variety of strategies and tactics – that will eventually evolve into a set of SRM "best practices" – that social risk managers should employ. Here are the major ones:

- *Don't (always) respond to influencers – especially with canned responses*

- *If engaging, be prepared and specific but avoid legal gray areas (policy, guarantees, etc. – plan responses as if they were press releases)*

- *Don't argue, remain neutral and calm, to not fuel the fire for all involved users*

- *Offer an apology – where appropriate – and try to move the conversation offline (or at least off the public sites)*

- *Follow strict social media policies and procedures that are corporate-wide*

- *Order ceases-and-desists through 3rd parties like Google to keep anonymity of the request users*

Activities & Capabilities

The first activity is *listening*. Companies need to listen to the social conversation diligently and as comprehensively as possible.

Wikipedia provides a list of social media applications/sites (at this point in time and as listed in Chapter 1). The number changes on a daily basis. The number of social media applications – and the creative use of user-created content – is changing as our understanding of social media evolves and as our creativity about social media applications grows.

Listening is complicated – and can yield enormous amounts of data that must be analyzed and stored. As suggested, companies have the option of developing their own listening/ analysis capabilities or outsourcing the activities to any number of vendors with the right capabilities. Our position is that unless a company plans to invest heavily in social media listening/analysis, it makes more sense to outsource the activities: it's hard to imagine a company declaring social media listening/analysis as a core competency.

The next activity is *analysis*.

As Chapters 1 and 2 suggest, an effective social media listening/analysis/engagement vendor (or in-house team) should be capable of answering the following questions:

- *Is data being converted into information and knowledge?*

- *Is the listening/ analysis solution capable of segmenting based on multiple interests?*

- *Does it provide clear action items? Can it answer questions?*

- *How comprehensive is the social data? How accurate is the data?*

- *How does the technology filter on phrases and remove irrelevant data?*

- *Does it use advanced natural language processing (NLP) such as "slop," "wildcards," punctuation, and compounded inclusions/ exclusions rule commands?*

- *What is a benchmark percentage for signal (versus noise) accuracy?*

- *How accurate is the basic sentiment analysis?*

- *Does the system have the ability to refine and continuously learn sentiment?*

- *Is sentiment based on the brand and/ or product, or generic sentence structure?*

- *How does the system apply analysis to punctuation?*

- *Is analysis based on sample data or all available data?*

- *How is influence measured and analyzed?*

- *How in-depth is the algorithm for making an influence assessment?*

- *Is influence determined in real-time?*

- *Can posts be filtered by influence level?*

- *Can you drill down in real-time?*

- *Can you search within the data for "what if" scenarios or are the data filters predefined?*

- *Can the listening/analysis solution filter by any combination of keyword, topic, sentiment, demographics, influencers, sources, and/or time?*

- *After filtering, does the system provide full access to underlying raw data?*

- *Can it uncover opportunities and spot threats?*

- *Is it intelligent enough to detect the unknowns and ensure timely awareness?*

- *Can the solution be distributed throughout the organization?*

- *Does it have corporate, role-based dashboards?*

- *Is it easy to use or does it require specialized skills and training?*

- *Can the system collect/filter/classify/structure/analyze in real-time?*

- *What are the time intervals for aggregating, filtering, analyzing and indexing data?*

- *How long is data stored and searchable (30 days, 6 months, a year)?*

This list of questions suggests that not all listening vendors are created equal and that it's important to understand your listening requirements (from your social media strategy) before selecting a partner. The list also suggests the range of talent companies need to develop in-house social media listening and analysis capabilities.

The next activity is SRM *engagement.* Here's the list of behaviors that companies should pursue:

- *Always try to take the conversation offline to control the spread*

- *Do not always engage, especially without preparation*

- *Do not discuss inflammatory topics on social media*

- *A profile used for business purposes should not have personal discussion*

- *Allow corporate communications to engage most frequently to make them the face of the company's Web presence*

- *Since taking down posts will often do more harm, use a 3rd party to order a cease and desist*

- *Assume anything posted on social media can be copied/shared and remain on the Internet forever*

- *Engage with influencers as soon as possible to resolve issues before their following becomes involved*

- *Use different tactics for risk and threat on social media than traditionally used for marketing and PR*

- *Once C-level executives become visible to the public on the Internet, assume they will always be visible*

- *Don't assume that someone with a large following is "influential"*

- *Assume that any social media account could belong to anyone in the world, including powerful people*

- *Remember that people hide their true identities to create a disconnect between their online and offline lives; they also often have multiple accounts on the same platform to separate their actions (ex. professional vs. personal vs. activist)*

- *Never assume that the conversation stops on one platform or with one person or group* ...

SRM Sectors & Roles

There are many business sectors that can benefit from SRM including:

- *Finance/Banking*

- *Pharmaceuticals*

- *Technology*

- *Energy & Utilities*

- *Retail*

- *Manufacturing (Auto, Food & Retail)*

- *Services* ...

Many of these sectors are highly regulated, sensitive to operational risk, associated to global activity and subject to scrutiny by investors and activists – and therefore candidates for *social risk intelligence* and *social risk management.*

Of the job responsibilities/titles, C-level and Board members are obvious consumers of SRM services. The following each have *risk, crisis management* or *threat* as a primary aspect of their job responsibility – and therefore candidates SRM:

- *Boards of Directors*

- *Chief Executives*

- *Chief Audit Officers*

- *Chief Compliance Officers*

- *Chief Financial Officers*

- *Chief Information Officers*

- *Chief Information Security Officers*

- *Chief Operating Officers*

- *Chief Risk Officers*

- *General Counsels*

- *Heads of HR*

- *Risk Managers*

- *Corporate Communications/PR*

- *Chief Marketing Officers*

When companies are monitoring real-time online discussions, they have the opportunity to receive an early detection of risks to which they can proactively respond. Some examples – that were missed – include:

- *In an online message board, an Eli Lilly sales representative anonymously discussed the practice of selling Zyprexa (an antipsychotic medicine) off-label for the treatment of dementia months before the news broke in the mainstream media.*

- *Nestle first came under criticism in online communities for sourcing palm oil (a main ingredient in many of its products, including Kit Kat and Nestle Crunch) from an Indonesian supplier accused of destroying rainforests. The company was eventually forced to issue a public apology and to restructure its supply chain to source from sustainable providers.*

- *Numerous employees have complained about their boss or their jobs on their personal Facebook page. One employee was fired after such an incident, but the latest court ruling as well as the National Labor Relations Board sided with the employee.*

- *Others have used Facebook and Twitter social networking sites to tout stocks in what proved to be a classic "pump and dump" fraud.*

- *Hospital employees have disseminated information over social media about patients, and doctors have used their cell phones to take photos of patients undergoing surgery and then posted them on social media sites.*

- *Risks are also embedded in what appear to be innocuous features of many social media tools. For example, an executive's Facebook or LinkedIn profile can potentially leak material of value to competitors who might be able to "mine" their contacts and posts to acquire inside information about the company's plans. Executives who use the TripIt feature of LinkedIn to announce where they will be traveling open themselves up to being followed.*

- *Allowing employee access to their personal Facebook, Twitter or other social media accounts from the company's internal server opens up numerous security and data privacy risks. People tend to be highly unsuspecting of the risks they can encounter in their ordinary use of social media.*

Social media has been around for nearly a decade, but we're still learning how to understand and control all of the indirect and indirect activity that defines social business intelligence. This is especially the case regarding SRM.

Chapter 5 - Conclusions

The promise of social business intelligence and social risk intelligence has turned the performance corner. While we're still cleaning, migrating and securing data, and worrying about platform compatibility, we've also connected social intelligence and risk intelligence to business performance management, a step that reflects rising expectations about what the end-game looks like. We've begun the journey toward structured/unstructured data integration/interpretation and real-time analytics – and also semantic processing, anticipating Web 3.0.

Avoiding #Fail is about management and mitigation. It's about social media policy and risk management. It's about resource allocation and corporate accountability. It's about image, reputation and brand management. It's about damage control. As the 100 disasters suggest, it's possible to get into a lot of trouble with social media. The social channel is an active channel that must be managed. If the 100 disasters don't convince you about the importance of social media and the risks surrounding the practice of social communication, then you're probably immune for just about every corporate danger. But if the 100 disasters convince you to pay close attention to social media, then *Avoiding #Fail* has done its job. Stay social, but stay safe.

About the Authors

Stephen J. Andriole is the Thomas G. Labrecque Professor of Business Technology at Villanova University where he teaches and directs applied research in business technology management. He is also a Fellow at the Cutter Consortium. He is formerly a Professor of Information Systems & Electrical & Computer Engineering at Drexel University and the George Mason Institute Professor and Chairman of the Department of Information Systems & Systems Engineering at George Mason University. Stephen J. Andriole was the Director of the Cybernetics Technology Office of the Defense Advanced Research Projects Agency (DARPA). He was also the Chief Technology Officer and Senior Vice President of Safeguard Scientifics, Inc. and the Chief Technology Officer and Senior Vice President for Technology Strategy at CIGNA Corporation.

Some of his thirty books include *Interactive Computer-Based Systems Design & Development* (Petrocelli Books, Inc., 1983), *Microcomputer Decision Support Systems* (QED Information Sciences, Inc., 1985), *Applications in Artificial Intelligence* (Petrocelli Books, Inc., 1986), *Information System Design Principles for the 90s* (AFCEA International Press, 1990), the *Sourcebook of Applied Artificial Intelligence* (McGraw-Hill, 1992), a (co-authored with Len Adelman) book on user interface technology for Lawrence Erlbaum Associates, Inc. entitled *Cognitive Systems Engineering* (1995), a book for McGraw-Hill entitled *Managing Systems Requirements: Methods, Tools & Cases* (1996), books on the *2nd Digital Revolution* (2005) and *Technology Due Diligence* (2009) – for IGI Press – and *Best Practices in Business Technology Management* (2009) and *IT's All About the People* (2011) for Auerbach Publications. He has published articles in the *Cutter IT Journal, Software Development, IEEE Software*, the *Communications of the ACM*, the *Communications of the AIS, IEEE IT Professional* and the *Journal of Information Technology Research*, among other journals. His *IT's All About the People* won the #4 spot for Best Business Technology Books in 2011 by CIO Insight Magazine.

Vincent J. Schiavone is the Co-Founder, Chairman and CEO of AKUDA LABS (akuda.com) and ListenLogic (ListenLogic.com), a pioneering "Social Business Intelligence" provider that delivers leading corporations with powerful insight from the rapidly expanding universe of customer comment and interaction to effectively understand and manage risk, reputation and customer engagement.

At the heart of ListenLogic is AKUDA LABS, a deep research and development team assembled from leading developers and experts from the public, private and academic sectors. AKUDA LABS is the developer of the state-of-the-art Pulsar Social Big Data Analytics Platform. Its extreme stream-data flow architecture gives companies the capability to collect, filter, structure and analyze social (and structured) data in real-time with upwards of an industry-leading one billion classified operations per second.

An entrepreneur, investor and author, Mr. Schiavone has created and grown a number of firms, driven by his commitment to helping create a platform for trust in the digital economy. Each of his companies has focused on one of the three elements: privacy, security and performance.

Mr. Schiavone focused first on privacy when he founded ePrivacy Group, a privacy consulting company and trusted email technology incubator. ePrivacy Group developed the framework and technology for a set of services like the Trusted Sender program, TEOS (a Trusted Email Open Standard), and SpamSquelcher.

This work led to the launch of TurnTide, an enterprise anti-spam technology company that was ultimately acquired by Symantec.

Security was the industry targeted by InfoSec Labs, a boutique consulting and training company serving global 2000 clients. InfoSec Labs was an early player in the security space providing assessments, penetration testing and strategy for its clients. InfoSec Labs pioneered practices still in use today and was acquired by SafeNet (SFNT).

In addition to his role at ListenLogic, Mr. Schiavone is a managing partner in the Acentio Group (acentio.com) which offers guidance on the optimization of business technology in medium-to-large sized enterprises, a senior consultant with Cutter Consortium (cutter.com), a strategic IT research and advisory firm and a managing partner at the investment firm Prioratus, LLC (prioratus.com).

Erika von Hoyer specializes in the development of cutting-edge methodologies for analyzing increasingly complex and diverse systems, converting big, dirty data into structured content for insights and predictive modeling. A strategic thinker with a pragmatic approach to problem solving, she has the ability to think laterally and to develop creative solutions to complex business issues. As the vice president of research and analytics for ListenLogic, Erika is responsible for advancing the technology and innovating new products by leading research at the intersection of statistics, evolutionary algorithm development, machine learning, and big data.

Initially responsible for advanced analytics (business intelligence, text mining, data visualization, and complex event processing) for hyperactive industries, she is now driving groundbreaking methodologies for threat mitigation solutions. Her work is to apprehend, explore, understand and report the power of asymmetric networks for the purposing of predicting tipping points and near term threats.

In 2006, Erika founded 360 Reputation, a boutique firm specializing in non-planned, custom research projects with a focus on stakeholder reputation and employee engagement. Identifying and improving internal reputation and intellectual capital is an area of expertise she first developed as vice president of marketing for SkillSurvey, a start-up HR technology company that pioneered automated reference checking as well as additional talent performance solutions.

Previously, Erika served as director of sales operations for Bentley Systems, a global provider of engineering software used for sustaining infrastructure. In this capacity, she was responsible for driving enhanced business decisions and overall business performance through data mining for market segmentation, multivariate statistical analysis, forecasting, modeling of customer value, loyalty and churn, scoring, pricing and return on employee investments.

Erika earned a dual BS degree in Education and English from Syracuse University and an Executive MBA degree from Villanova University where she now serves as board member for the alumni association.

Mark D. Langsfeld is an expert in social media and business intelligence. He advises large enterprises on how to manage risk, engage with customers and drive innovation. He is the Co-Founder and Chief Strategy Officer of AKUDA LABS and ListenLogic.

AKUDA LABS (akuda.com) is revolutionizing real-time, streaming big data filtering, classification and analytics. Its proprietary Pulsar hypercomputing platform is the fastest, most efficient real-time streaming classification engine available, processing 500 million streaming classification operations per second (SCOPS) on a path to 1+ billion SCOPS.

ListenLogic (ListenLogic.com) is the leading streaming big data business intelligence provider delivering companies real-time monitoring of risks and opportunities and deep inspection of markets and products out of social media chaos. ListenLogic serves as an ongoing proof point for Pulsar's incredible hypercomputing technology.

Previously, he was the Co-Founder of Mediagistics, a search analytics and arbitrage company. Prior to that he served as Vice President of New Products at Move, Inc. He was also Vice President of Product Strategy for 4anything.com. He was also a Financial Analyst at BT Alex Brown in the Real Estate Investment Banking Group.

Mark R. Harrington is an accomplished, versatile marketer. Mark's unique expertise spans publishing to payments and education to ecommerce. He's excelled in Inc. 500s to Fortune 500s and has been instrumental in landmark exits worth over a half billion dollars, helping catapult an array of pioneering industry solutions. He is CMO of AKUDA LABS and ListenLogic.

As Client Delivery Head on Citi Prepaid's Management Team he led Marketing, Design, Implementation and Client Services for clients like Apple, BMW, Disney, Google, P&G and Verizon. He helped drive revenue 36x, sat on Citi's Global Marketing Council and Social Media Committee and was GM for Ecount's $220MM Citi acquisition, receiving the Bertie-Bob Leadership Award.

As Half.com's co-founder and youngest Management Team member, he ran Retention Marketing, managing 75% of gross merchandise sales. Acquired by eBay for $350MM, Half hit profitability largely due to his pioneering of the P2P textbook market, earning him eBay's Out of This World Award. He also helped devise "one of the greatest publicity coups in history" (*Time Magazine*) Half.com, Oregon.

At Infonautics he co-founded Company Sleuth (*PC Magazine* Top 100) and Sports Sleuth (Yahoo! Top 50), earning him their Innovation Award. At Pearson he promoted four national Top 10 higher ed titles earning him their Summit Award.

He holds a BS in Marketing, Honors with Distinction, from The Pennsylvania State University Smeal College of Business and was a Melbourne Wesley Cummings and Dorothy M. Kelly Scholar.